Perceptual Drift

Perceptual Drift
BLACK ART AND AN ETHICS OF LOOKING

KEY JO LEE

With contributions by
ERICA MOIAH JAMES
ROBIN COSTE LEWIS
CHRISTINA SHARPE

The Cleveland Museum of Art
Distributed by Yale University Press, New Haven and London

THIS PUBLICATION IS MADE POSSIBLE IN PART BY THE ANDREW W. MELLON FOUNDATION

Made possible with support from the Andy Warhol Foundation for the Visual Arts.

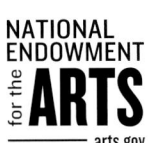

This project is supported in part by an award from the National Endowment for the Arts.

© 2022 The Cleveland Museum of Art

All rights reserved. No part of the contents of this book may be reproduced, in whole or in part, including illustrations, in any form (beyond that permitted by Sections 107 and 108 of the US Copyright Law and except by reviewers for the public press), without written permission from the Cleveland Museum of Art. The works of art themselves may be protected by copyright and may not be reproduced in any form or medium without the permission of the copyright holders.

Images of the works of art in the exhibition were provided by the lenders, unless otherwise noted.

All text by Robin Coste Lewis is © Robin Coste Lewis.

All text by Christina Sharpe is © Christina Sharpe.

Objects in the collection of the Cleveland Museum of Art were photographed by museum photographers Howard Agriesti, David Brichford, and Gary Kirchenbauer. James Kohler prepared the digital files. The museum holds copyright to its images. When known, other copyright holders and photographers are acknowledged in the captions.

Library of Congress Control Number: 2022938923
ISBN 978-0-300-26392-3

All measurements are in centimeters; height precedes width precedes depth.

Tom Barnard, Director of Publications
Rachel Beamer, Publication Project Manager
Edited by Amanda Glesmann
Proofread by Amy Sparks
Designed by John Brown VI

The Cleveland Museum of Art
11150 East Boulevard
Cleveland, OH 44106-1797
www.clevelandart.org

Distributed by
Yale University Press
302 Temple Street
P.O. Box 209040
New Haven, CT 06520-9040
www.yalebooks.com/art

Jacket: **Bouffant Pride** (detail), 2003. Ellen Gallagher (American, b. 1965). Collage of photogravures, plasticine, paint, ink, and found objects; support: rag paper; sheet: 34.3 x 26.6 cm. The Cleveland Museum of Art, Judith and James Saks in memory of Lynn and Dr. Joseph Tomarkin Endowment, 2003.340. © Ellen Gallagher. Courtesy Gagosian.

6	**DIRECTOR'S FOREWORD**	
	William M. Griswold	
7	**ACKNOWLEDGMENTS**	
	Key Jo Lee	
9	**INTRODUCTION**	
	Key Jo Lee	
15	**"TO DECODE THE FULL SPECTRUM": JACK WHITTEN'S *RHO I***	
	Christina Sharpe	
33	**AN APPROACH TO LORNA SIMPSON'S *CURE/HEAL***	
	Key Jo Lee	
49	**"SPIT-BITE"**	
	NOTES IN CONVERSATION WITH ELLEN GALLAGHER'S *BOUFFANT PRIDE*: AN INTRODUCTION	
	Robin Coste Lewis	
63	**A GUST OF GRACE: SIMONE LEIGH'S *LAS MENINAS***	
	Erica Moiah James	
80	**THE CLEVELAND MUSEUM OF ART BOARD OF TRUSTEES**	

DIRECTOR'S FOREWORD
WILLIAM M. GRISWOLD

The Cleveland Museum of Art (CMA) is entering its second century, carrying forward its mission to serve all people through its collection and programs. As we contemplate the many issues of our time, we must consider how we prepare ourselves to fully engage a broad and diverse audience with works of art that complicate or challenge the historical narratives that we have come to know. *Perceptual Drift: Black Art and an Ethics of Looking* offers several innovative modes of interrogation that reflect the transformational possibilities of art to which this museum is dedicated. *Perceptual Drift* emphasizes the importance of intellectual and physical openness to building honest and impactful relationships with art and with our audiences, especially when contending with works that confront painful histories that have been otherwise erased or concealed. In *Perceptual Drift*, each contributing scholar presents a unique framework for encountering formally and conceptually complex artworks from the CMA's collection of works by African American artists. The methods of interpretation demonstrated in this volume—historical and archival research, connoisseurship, memoir, and nonlinear narrative—all espouse the generative quality of a bodily encounter as the basis for analysis. In other words, these essays attest to the importance of bodily presence to enhancing perception.

For their support in making *Perceptual Drift* possible, I would like to express my deepest gratitude to the National Endowment for the Arts, as well as to the Andrew W. Mellon Foundation. Growing the African American art collection at the CMA and generating new scholarship on its holdings are major goals expressed in the museum's strategic and diversity, equity, and inclusion plans. Key Jo Lee, associate curator of American art, has gathered together a group of authors from the fields of art history, creative writing, and literary theory. These include Dr. Erica Moiah James, assistant professor of art and art history at the University of Miami; Dr. Robin Coste Lewis, recipient of the 2022 Joseph Brodsky Rome Prize for Poetry and writer-in-residence at the University of Southern California; and Dr. Christina Sharpe, professor and Canada Research Chair in Black Studies in the Humanities at York University. Through their astute and innovative writing, these authors illuminate and respond both to our visitors' calls for more information about the CMA's holdings and to an institutional desire to forefront works of art and perspectives relevant to our time.

I am grateful for the collaborative spirit across the museum's editorial and design staff, and extend particular thanks to Heidi Strean, chief exhibition, design, and publications officer, and Tom Barnard, director of publications, for their tireless efforts. Finally, I thank all of the artists whose work appears in these pages, for it is they who inspire us all.

William M. Griswold
Director and President
Sarah S. and Alexander M. Cutler Chair
The Cleveland Museum of Art

ACKNOWLEDGMENTS
KEY JO LEE

I am truly grateful to the Cleveland Museum of Art (CMA) for providing space and resources for this experiment. My deepest appreciation is extended to the many people who have generously offered their advice, intellectual and moral support, and friendship over the course of this project. I hope this book pulsates with the curiosity and generosity that each author brought to it.

Great thanks must go to the incredible artists and their representatives who have allowed us to make their work a part of this project. This publication would have been impossible otherwise. The exceptional contributions of Dr. Erica Moiah James, Dr. Robin Coste Lewis, and Dr. Christina Sharpe were also essential. Their scholarship and ways of being in the world have inspired my path. I am very grateful for the intellectual legacies instilled by my friend and mentor Elizabeth Alexander, who epitomizes a life well-lived, as well as for Dr. Kobena Mercer and Dr. Alexander Nemerov, whose innovative scholarship and personal guidance have shaped my trajectory. At Colby College, the Colby Museum of Art, and the Lunder Institute for American Art, I thank Dr. Tanya Sheehan, who has been shepherding my scholarship since I was an undergraduate, and who invited me to apply for the fellowship that inspired this book. I also thank Dr. Sharon Corwin, then the Colby Museum of Art's director and chief curator, and my fellowship cohort, Dr. Adrienne L. Childs, Dr. Tess Korobkin, Dr. Anna Arabindan-Kesson, Dr. Rebecca VanDiver, and Dr. John Ott, whose keen minds productively tested my thinking. Incredible gratitude goes to Olivia Hochstadt, who never complained about the wild research journey with which she was tasked.

The executive team and staff at the CMA deserve exceptional thanks. The support I have received from every level of the institution cannot be overstated. Particular gratitude is extended to William Griswold, the museum's president and director; Heidi Strean, chief exhibition, design, and publications officer; Heather Lemonedes Brown, Virginia N. and Randall J. Barbato Deputy Director and Chief Curator; and Jennifer DePrizio, chief learning officer, public and academic engagement, for their enthusiasm about this project from the beginning. In publications, I thank Rachel Beamer, our steadfast publication project manager, and Tom Barnard, director of publications, for their unending patience and support on this project. I also thank John Brown VI, associate publications designer, for his gorgeous book design. I extend appreciation to Amanda Glesmann for her expert editing and to Amy Sparks for proofreading. I also thank my curatorial colleagues Mark Cole, chair of modern, contemporary, and decorative art and William P. and Amanda C. Madar Curator of American Painting and Sculpture; Emily Liebert, curator of contemporary art; Nadiah Rivera Fellah, associate curator of contemporary art; Emily Peters, curator of prints and drawings; and Britany Salisbury, associate curator of prints and drawings, for sharing their insights on individual artworks. I am grateful to Kikesa Kimbwala DeRobles, director's fellow extraordinaire, whose research assistance was essential. A very special and loud thank you must go to Hannah Hilditch, academic programs coordinator, without whose steadfast support in all aspects of my work at the museum I would have been lost.

Last but certainly not least, I thank my family and friends. Kathy and Nate, you are always, always in my corner, and I don't know where I would be without you. Noah, Isabel, and Clio, you are the greatest gift I've ever received. Gigi, Pancho, Adriana, Dave, Bert, and Nicole, you expanded my family and heart in ways I hadn't imagined. Andria, Carmen, and Kerry, you made Cleveland feel like home. Oana and Claire, you rescued me. Barney . . . always.

Key Jo Lee
Associate Curator of American Art
The Cleveland Museum of Art

8

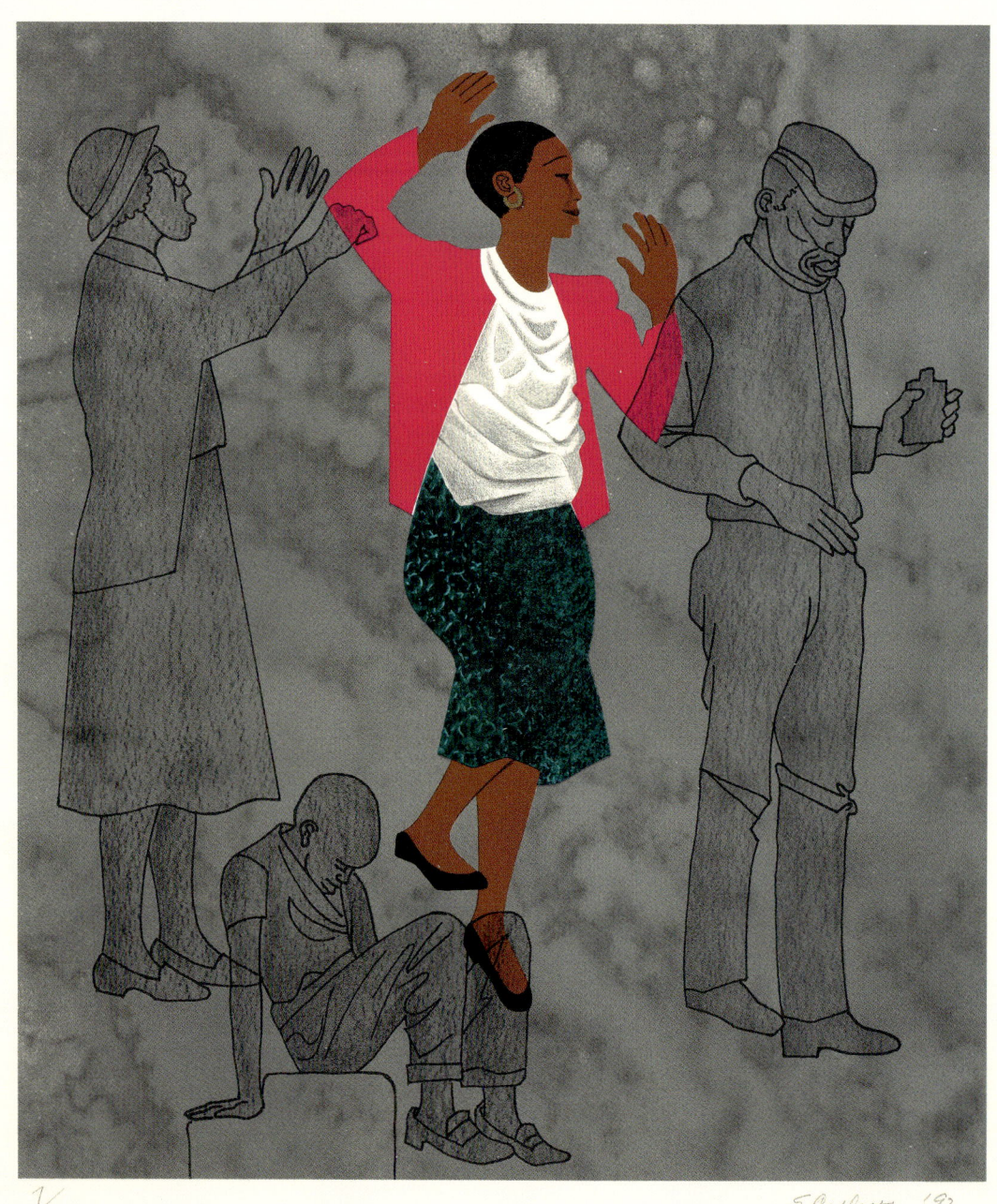

INTRODUCTION
DEFINING PERCEPTUAL DRIFT
KEY JO LEE

I chose rather to focus on how to create nonracist, yet race-specific literature within an already race-inflected language for readers who have been forced to deal with assumptions of racial hierarchy. I chose to write as though there were nothing to prove or disprove, as though an unraced world already existed. Not to transcend race, or to aspire to some fraudulent "universalism"—a code word that had come to mean "nonblack"— but to claim the liberty of my own imagination. For I have never lived, nor has anyone, in a world in which race did not matter.
—Toni Morrison, *The Source of Self-Regard*[1]

Introduction

"This story is told from inside the circle."[2] Very early in her book *Wayward Lives, Beautiful Experiments: Intimate Histories of Riotous Black Girls, Troublesome Women, and Queer Radicals*, literary theorist Saidiya Hartman uses this phrase to describe her method of "close narration," which "places the voice of the narrator and character in inseparable relation, so that the vision, language, and rhythms of the wayward shape and arrange the text." The assembly of essays herein is also narrated from this special kind of "inside." And so . . . these stories are told from inside the circle, from a space of affective encounter, which I understand as sensing even the most miniscule contours of encounter between and among bodies. It emerges from a desire to articulate a framework, however contingent and fine, that forefronts the multidirectional, multimodal, and polydimensional perspectual field necessary to plumb the occlusions and obscurities in the archive in order to narrate histories that attend to subjectivities and stories that are inconvenient to persistent master narratives because they make demands, assert refusals, and at times actually force us to move in our attempts to apprehend. In other words, they ask us to willingly drift openly *in order to* perceive that which is "inside." In doing so, these pages are the fruition of a precariously held dream to put forth a text that poetically marries theories and methods for apprehending art that involve the entire body, that offers ways of engaging complex artworks that rely on both historical and embodied knowledge, and that opens new pathways of inquiry for every reader.

Guiding both new and seasoned museum visitors through different approaches to close-looking has been one of the most rewarding aspects of my career. I've been trained in multiple techniques, both as an art historian and as a gallery teacher, to lead individuals and groups toward greater sensory literacy and critical descriptive and interpretive skills. I began this training in graduate school, under the auspices of the Wurtele Gallery Teacher Program, in a generously endowed gallery teacher position at the Yale University Art Gallery. There I was trained in Visual Thinking Strategies (VTS), an open-ended interrogative process of interpreting artwork that is accessible and effective for audiences of all ages and skill levels. Collectively, the gallery teachers saw thousands of K-12 and adult groups each year. During this time I also trained to lead sessions for adults with memory loss, vision loss, and various neurodivergencies. Given my academic concentration on the history of art and African American studies, I was often called upon

Untitled: Walking Blindly, 1992. Elizabeth Catlett (American, 1915–2012). Color lithograph; sheet: 57.8 x 47.3 cm. The Cleveland Museum of Art, John L. Severance Fund and Richard Florsheim Art Fund, 1994.304.3. © 2022 Mora-Catlett Family / Licensed by VAGA at Artists Rights Society (ARS), New York.

to assist viewers in locating and recognizing Black artists and narratives and, in the case of specialized sessions for medical students, in techniques for recognizing both helpful and harmful biases. These experiences enriched my scholarly work in that they helped me to understand how necessary it is to activate all means of perception in any interpretive engagement with an artwork. They also sharpened my ability to facilitate productive interactions with complex and painful American histories within artworks through activities and thought experiments that increase receptiveness and rigor simultaneously. Such a necessary concurrence of bodily receptiveness and intellectual rigor characterizes perceptual drift.

I developed the concept of "perceptual drift" over the course of a year-long research fellowship at the Lunder Institute for American Art at Colby College in Waterville, Maine. In combining the word "perceptual," which describes the realm of perception, apprehension, assessment, or interpretation, and the word "drift," which is defined as a driving movement or force—as in to be carried along by currents of water or air, or by the force of circumstances; to wander—but also as the meaning or intent of a thing, perceptual drift is an apt framework for the Black feminist new materialist methods herein. The approaches represented in the following essays are integrative, interdisciplinary, and intersensory. They destabilize the hierarchy between viewer and object by recognizing an artwork's agentive nature, or its ability to impact and prioritize materiality, or how and of what something is made and experienced, or how a work acts as a body engaged with ours. They also deemphasize strict temporal linearity—though it is present—while emphasizing other resonant connections. They show that perceptual drift is not a singularly authored idea; rather, it is a useful umbrella under which we can nurture an ethical mode of addressing art and history that makes the scholar's positionality plain and deeply considers a work's materiality as an arbiter of meaning.

Perceptual drift is governed by five principles of engagement: intention, slow and multisensory attention (or close-looking, reflexivity), overt self-consciousness, collaborative meaning-making, and disciplinary openness. Each of the four authors' methods epitomizes these five principles in some way. In our contributions to this volume, art historian and curator Erica Moiah James, poet and essayist Robin Coste Lewis, literary theorist Christina Sharpe, and I are each invested in an interpretive process that places us in a direct relationship with our object of inquiry. As a matter of interest and expertise, this book is primarily concerned with the artistic production of Black artists working and living in the United States, though the artists and artworks brought into context are varied. We have each expanded, in our own way, on a single work of art from the collection of the Cleveland Museum of Art (CMA). Each meditation, for that is what these essays represent, is steeped in multisensorial resonances and intertextual complexities. Every essay asks how we might trace the "wayward," or those persons, things, and experiences that might otherwise go missing from historical records and accounts, and each offers an approach to "looking," or analysis and interpretation, that can aid a relationship to any work of art.[3] Here, however, the methodologies utilized specifically serve artworks and artists who aim at the historical lacunae—and the complicated means of access—that characterize works contending with Black American subjectivities.

This study is specific in that it centers on a very few CMA artworks. Each author's meditation is discursive in approach, and each offers a guide to assessing and responding to their subject's sensory demands. Overall, these texts are a considered response to questions and ideas that I've fielded for over a decade as a museum educator. Collectively, they correspond to my personal, curatorial, and scholarly ethos, which is steeped in the desire to serve people and stories that have previously been rendered invisible, and to recognize the non-neutral and strenuous yet rewarding nature of that work. As such, this book demonstrates ways of being with art that combine multivalent engagements with dominant theories of art and of history and an investment in Black feminist and new materialist critiques of those theories. As a framework, perceptual drift demonstrates that the inseparability of the act of aesthetic apprehension is equally ruled by the forces of human and objective agency. It relies on the notion that objects, or "things," are in a nonhierarchical and reciprocal relationship, one that is foundational to an ethics of aesthetic engagement that is always necessary but especially so when one turns one's attention to that which is lost to, or lies in excess of, conventional archives—as Black subjectivities so often do. But what does it mean to say that this slim but potent volume is undergirded by Black feminist new materialist impulses, and why is this essential?

BLACK FEMINIST NEW MATERIALISM

Philosophical materialism dictates that everything we can perceive through our senses is material and that that which we cannot sense does not exist or impact worldly processes. This idea tends to create a dichotomy between what exists tangibly and what does not. Following this separation is the distinction between organic and inorganic material, the difference between living matter (e.g., animals) and nonliving matter (e.g., stone). Additionally, materialist thought holds that this is a binary that cannot be blurred, that a living thing is agentival and a nonliving entity is not, thus establishing an impenetrable hierarchy. In contrast, new materialism aligns itself against the centralization of human agency by undermining the materialist notion that only living things have agency and that there is an inherent and unchangeable hierarchy among agentive beings.

For example, political theorist Jane Bennett offers a way out of the bind of subject-object disparity by espousing a vitalist approach that disavows a separation between person and thing, breaking the bonds of purely dialectical thinking that persistently obtain in intellectual discussions of materiality wherein there is always the possibility of demystifying matter. She maintains a wariness of demystification, as it "presumes that at the heart of any event or process lies a *human* agency that has illicitly been projected onto things."[4] Differing from traditional vitalism, which posits an animating "spirit" that separates the living from the nonliving, Bennett calls for a vitalism that "equates affect with materiality, rather than posit[ing] a separate force that can enter and animate a physical body."[5] She joins this version with a nondialectical materialism à la Democritus, Epicurus, Spinoza, Diderot, and Deleuze, advocating a "material vitality" that privileges "the capacity of things . . . not only to impede or block the will and designs of humans but also to act as quasi agents or forces with trajectories, propensities, or tendencies of their own."[6] In other words, Bennett endorses the possibility of a material or nonhuman agency as at least partly constituent in any encounter, while noting that the ability to discover or sense those agencies requires effort. She writes, "The capacity to detect the presence of impersonal affect requires that one is caught up in it. One needs, at least for a while, to suspend suspicion and adopt a more open-ended comportment."[7] With perceptual drift, I take up Bennett's new materialist claims of a lively, yet unsouled, vitality of things and her call for the openness necessary for its detection.

In her essay "The Social Construction of Black Feminist Thought," Patricia Hill Collins describes the foundational differences between white and Black feminist thought. Collins, a social theorist and scholar of African American studies, points out that Black feminist thought takes into consideration the interlocking structures of race, gender, and class, while their white counterparts did not generally have to consider the impact of race, especially their own, on their desired outcomes. She also highlights the differences between the positions of Black men and women, observing that Black men could focus on the intersections of race and class without necessarily considering the impact of their gender on their desired outcomes. The result is that Black women occupy a unique space of "both/or," which Collins describes as "being both a member of a group and yet standing apart from it."[8] This sui generis positionality requires alternative modes of resistance. As Collins writes, "Like other subordinate groups, African American women not only have developed distinctive interpretations of black women's oppression but have done so by using alternative ways of producing and validating knowledge itself."[9] This doesn't necessarily produce a more accurate understanding of oppression, however—that would "suggest that oppression can be quantified and compared and that adding layers of oppression produces a potentially clearer standpoint." Rather, Collins sites the potency of Black feminist thought, which is always already occupying multiple consciousnesses governed by the intersectional identities of Black women. Importantly, due to this unique positionality, Black feminist epistemologies, or ways of knowing and determinations of what can be known, are distinct. This, along with the broad and deep gaps in the collection of historical documents and records of Black women's subjectivity in the United States, which are rooted in oral and embodied knowledge transfer, means that Black feminist approaches to narrating history require that we view our bodies and experiences, and those of our foremothers, as archives to be plumbed, and that we acknowledge that the methods for doing so are varied. Together, Black feminist thought and new materialism provide a useful theoretical basis for the ideas and methods that are the connective tissue of perceptual drift.

ARTICULATIONS OF PERCEPTUAL DRIFT

As I selected the artwork on which each author would meditate, I was driven toward pieces that seem to actively resist easy interpretation. Ranging in date from 1977 to 2019, the works are disparate in medium and genre but are characterized by a common conceptual complexity that speaks directly to nuanced histories, archival erasures or oppressions, and previously occluded interpretations. As such, they demand multiperspectival and multisensorial engagement for revelation. Each piece insists on an ethics of engagement that cannot be purely intellectual. This set of moral governing principles requires of its viewers a physical and intellectual fluidity of the kind that is always necessary when one turns one's attention to that which is lost to, or lies in excess of, conventional narratives—as Black subjectivities so often do. These essays make visible un- or underacknowledged histories. And while each author expresses these fundamentals of perceptual drift differently, all four essays take up the idea of freedom in fugitivity.

In the opening essay, Christina Sharpe's "'To decode the full spectrum': Jack Whitten's *Rho I*" illuminates Whitten's monumental monochromatic painting *Rho I* (1977) by exploring his theories of art making and his desire to show that abstraction could be a tool to create a nonhierarchical, and perhaps inseparable, subjectivity belonging to himself and the work of art simultaneously. Sharpe considers every aspect of the work's making, placing it and Whitten in nonlinear relation to other freedom-seeking artists from multiple generations and marking a legacy of spatial considerations of architectures of Black liberation.

Next, "Liberatory Dissemblance: An Approach to Lorna Simpson's *Cure/Heal*," I contemplate the freedom-making possibilities intrinsic to concealment and conceptual opacity to advance a multisensory, archival, and embodied analysis of Simpson's tenebrous 1990s lithograph of unworn suede pumps on a velvet ground. My interpretation reflects on Black women's political "culture of dissemblance," a concept outlined by Black feminist historian Darlene Clark Hine in her seminal essay "Rape and the Inner Lives of Black Women in the Middle West: Preliminary Notes on the Culture of Dissemblance." As Hine explains, "in the face of pervasive stereotypes and negative estimations of the sexuality of black women, it was imperative that they collectively create alternative self-images [to] shield from scrutiny these private, empowering definitions of self."[10] The liberatory dissemblance to which the essay refers expands Hine's notion beyond its geographic and historical specificity, demonstrating how it informs both Simpson's artistic practice and my scholarly practice, each of us refusing to pretend at neutrality and depersonalization and exploring the importance of concealment to revolutionary apprehension.

In "Spit-Bite: Notes and Conversation with Ellen Gallagher's *Bouffant Pride*, an Introduction," Black people's hair as concept and concrete form are at the nexus of Robin Coste Lewis's poetic study of Gallagher's discreetly sized multimedia collage *Bouffant Pride* (2003), in which a 1970s advertisement for women's and men's wigs is remade into a layering of inter- and intracultural signifiers of difference and belonging using photogravure, yellow plasticine clay, paint, ink, found objects. Lewis offers a personal and intertextual reflection on the mysteries and miracles of Black inheritances of hair as historical artifact and on herself as an assemblage, or "marriage of politics, philosophy, aesthetics."[11] Specifically, this suite of poems attends to the elemental power invested in a single hairstyle: the bouffant.

Finally, Erica Moiah James, in her essay "A Gust of Grace: Simone Leigh's *Las Meninas*," takes up and further globalizes Darlene Clark Hine's notion of dissemblance as she posits Leigh's clay and raffia figural sculpture as "fugitive" and a "super metaobject." Drawing on theorist W. J. T. Mitchell's notion of a "metapicture," which doesn't "just illustrate theories of picturing and vision [but also] show[s] us what vision is, and picture theory," James guides through the work's "condition of uncertainty," or fugitivity, and the ways it "can be seen as a sanctuary for the historically oppressed and marginalized."[12] Ultimately, James's tracing of the temporal, geographical, and perspectival slippages within Leigh's *Las Meninas* reveals the capaciousness of meaning that this fugitivity affords.

Ultimately, my hope is that within the essays in *Perceptual Drift: Black Art and an Ethics of Looking* you will find not only new understandings of these artists and artworks but also new ways of thinking about and being with all art. It is important to note that the strategies employed here aren't limited to Black art, nor are they limited to scholars. Everyone can adopt the principles of vulnerability and receptiveness inherent in perceptual drift.

1. Toni Morrison, *The Source of Self-Regard: Selected Essays, Speeches, and Meditations* (New York: Knopf, 2019), 198.

2. Saidiya V. Hartman, *Wayward Lives, Beautiful Experiments: Intimate Histories of Riotous Black Girls, Troublesome Women, and Queer Radicals* (New York: Norton, 2020), xv.

3. I acknowledge the ableist tenor of "looking"; however, in perceptual drift "looking" is shorthand for the kind of multisensory encounter encouraged by the method. The quotations are meant to indicate this conceptual slippage.

4. Jane Bennett, *Vibrant Matter: A Political Ecology of Things* (Durham, NC: Duke University Press, 2011), xiv.

5. Ibid.

6. Ibid., viiii.

7. Ibid., xv.

8. Patricia Hill Collins, "The Social Construction of Black Feminist Thought," in *The Black Feminist Reader*, ed. Joy James and T. Denean Sharpley-Whiting (Malden, MA: Blackwell, 2000), 191.

9. Ibid., 183.

10. Darlene Clark Hine, "Rape and the Inner Lives of Black Women in the Middle West: Preliminary Thoughts on the Culture of Dissemblance," in *Words of Fire: An Anthology of African American Feminist Thought*, ed. Beverly Guy-Sheftall (New York: New Press, 1995), 383.

11. See Robin Coste Lewis, "Spit-Bite: Notes and Conversation with Ellen Gallagher's *Bouffant Pride*, an Introduction," page 50 in this volume.

12. See Erica Moiah James, "A Gust of Grace: Simone Leigh's *Las Meninas*," pages 64–65 in this volume..

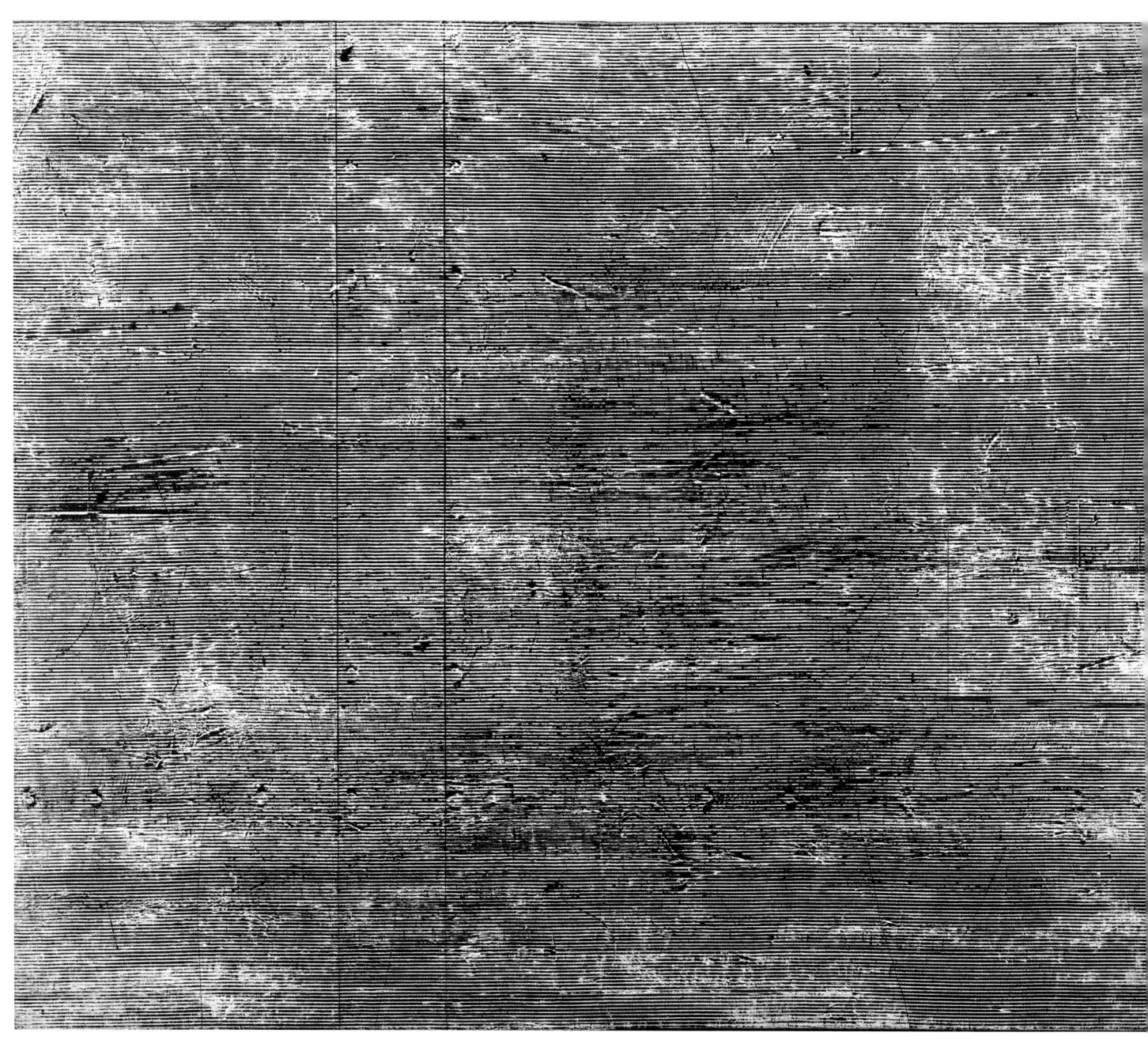

"TO DECODE THE FULL SPECTRUM": JACK WHITTEN'S *RHO I*
CHRISTINA SHARPE

I. "A WORD IN YOUR MOUTH"

In a conversation with Jack Whitten in 2008, curator Stuart Horodner asked a series of questions—ones that were often posed to the artist—about his relationship to the US South, about growing up there under segregation in the 1940s and 1950s, and about what sent him north, to art school at the Cooper Union in New York. Whitten started his answer by talking about what he termed "Southern sensibility" and its un- or under-observed impact in the visual (as opposed to the literary) arts. He went on to speak of himself as a young person who occasionally made pocket money by hunting and skinning muskrats, raccoons, possums, and other small animals in and around his hometown of Bessemer, Alabama, and drying and selling their hides. He then asked his interviewer, and by extension the listening audience, "Do you have any idea how that has affected my thinking about materials?"[1] (Do we have any idea how this affected his thinking about surfaces?) Raised in an environment where he learned how to make what was needed from watching his mother and others had a profound effect on how Whitten thought about materials, how he understood how to work them, and how he understood the properties and possibilities of collage, space, projection, ecology, depth, surface, cosmology, and cosmogony.

Horodner's questions invited a rehearsal of autobiography and, perhaps more specifically, an inventory of his experiences as a young Black man coming of age in the segregated South. In his answers, Whitten was both contained and richly detailed. Contained because he refused to recount a set of traumatic events. He was emphatic about this, saying: "I have some horrible memories that I don't even feel comfortable talking about in person. And why should I? . . . I insist upon living in the now. . . . I can't afford to carry that baggage."[2] Such demands for an autobiographical narrative that is external to the work of the painting are often repeated. But it seems to me that so much of what Whitten had to say about this time, about its effects on him and the ways they lingered into the present, is to be found in the trajectory of his experimentation (that Southern sensibility), in the materials he used and how he used them—found, in other words, in the work itself. When he asked, "Do you have any idea . . .?" he was speaking into the space of vocabularies and cosmologies that are known, studied, and made by the various communities that he was a part of but that have remained opaque in many ideologies, practices, and histories of painting.

Whitten's answers to the questions were measured, fleshed out by time, and filled in with his own counter invitation to consider the gift(s) of a Black Southern culture that is organized around three institutions without which he said he would not have survived—family, church, and school. He detailed what that grounding had meant to him, the richness that it imparted, and what he carried with him of it to his present work. And he was very clear that it *was* Black Southern cultures (and also African cultures) that guided his work. That specificity is key. It informed a story he told about encountering a new definition of the picture plane when he arrived in New York, started art classes at the Cooper Union, and began having conversations with a wide and diverse circle of artists. Whitten said that as young people, he and his friends "skinned raccoons flat against the wall" and experimented with and drew on those dried skins; this produced in him

FIGURE 1
Rho I, 1977. Jack Whitten. (American, 1939–2018). Acrylic on canvas; 192.8 x 213.2 cm. The Cleveland Museum of Art, Gift of Scott C. Mueller and Margaret Fulton Mueller, 2010.1. © Jack Whitten Estate. Courtesy the Estate and Hauser & Wirth.

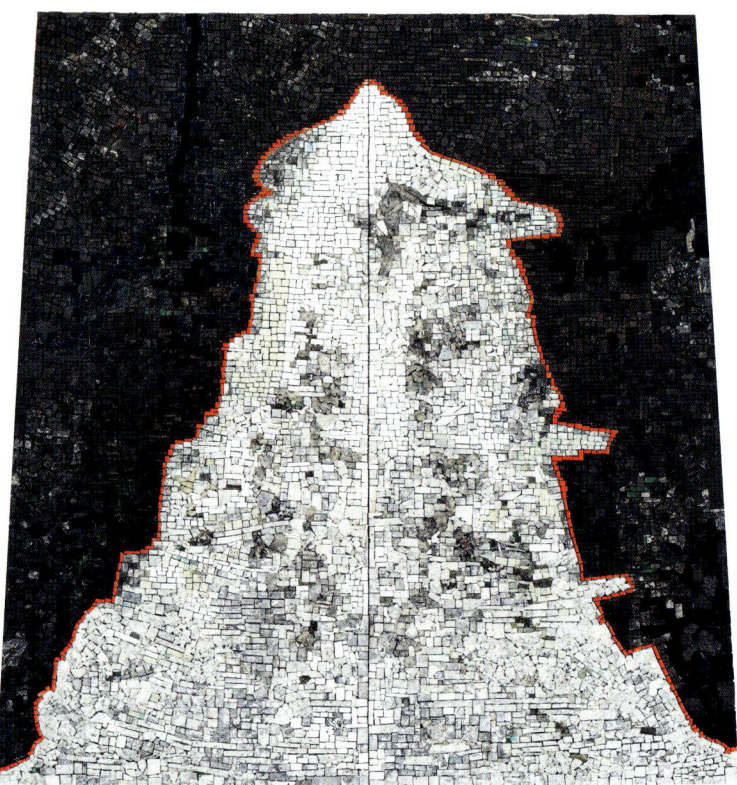
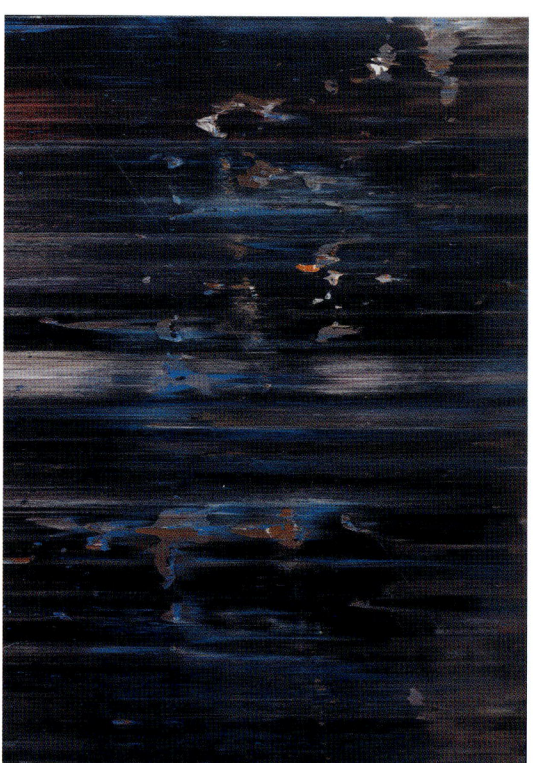

FIGURE 2
Black Monolith IV For Jacob Lawrence, 2001. Jack Whitten. Acrylic on canvas; 243.8 × 243.8 cm. Mott-Warsh Collection, Flint, Michigan. © Jack Whitten Estate. Courtesy the Estate and Hauser & Wirth.

FIGURE 3
April's Shark, 1974. Jack Whitten. Acrylic on canvas; 182.9 × 132 cm. © Jack Whitten Estate. Courtesy the Estate and Hauser & Wirth. Photo: Jeff McLane.

a *specific* relation to the picture plane. The skin was his plane, and Whitten delivered an entire lesson in surface, tactility, innovation, material, and use. The work then, and his commitment to the now, to inhabiting the complex present, was always already the answer to any questions about how he experienced antiblackness [fig. 2] "The political," as Whitten said, "is in the work. I know it's in there because I put it in there."[3] Add to this Whitten's commitments to the spiritual as practice and material. As he wrote in his studio notes, "My paintings are designed as weapons. Their objective is to penetrate and destroy the Western aesthetic."[4]

In an earlier interview in *BOMB* magazine, Whitten talked about transformation, materials, and process: "Transformation is very important. Materials are just raw materials, that's all. It's like a word, anybody can have access to the same word, but a word in your mouth is totally different from a word in mine."[5] This points to a corollary movement in the worlds of Black literature. Points to writers like Toni Morrison, Toni Cade Bambara, Michele Wallace, Gayl Jones, and Alice Walker, who experiment with form and subject, with questions of Blackness, gender, slavery, settler colonialism, imperialism, sex, and gender. These writers were aware of one another, and they were speaking to one another through their work and their desire to illuminate the particularities, commonalities, and specificities of Blackness as they saw them. They were in their time and also ahead of their time. This is a response to a call for a certain language of writing and painting understood to be political—readily available and legible, because people had learned to read it—a narrative and gestural visual vocabulary. With Whitten's "a word in your mouth is totally different from a word in mine," he joined the hand to the tongue, and language to material, as he worked through questions of perception, gesture, and the multiple languages of world and art making. To use that simile "like a word" when referring to the physical and the tactile, to paint, surface, and wood, demonstrated that for Whitten, the materials were of course necessary but also secondary, or even tertiary, to what one does with them, what sensibilities and ambitions one brings to them, and how they make and shape. The materials are the stuff by which transformation occurs [fig. 3]. As one critic has noted, Whitten "transforms the materials from what we expect them to do, so we look at paint differently."[6]

II. *RHO I*

Rho I (1977) is large; it measures nearly seventy-two by eighty-four inches. It is part of Whitten's Greek Alphabet series of paintings that he made between 1976 and 1979, in which he completely removed the color spectrum to see how black and white can and do work together. In this series of paintings he also moved from oil paints to faster-drying acrylics. He turned his attention to the materiality of the paint, in the process removing the hand and "relational thinking" from the work. He wanted to "take gesture in another direction."[7]

Whitten described himself as moving toward the gray and toward new possibility—not either/or or both/and but neither/nor. He explained that he was looking for some new space, some new method: "[In] the Greek Alphabet series . . . [w]hat I discovered is that philosophically I don't like either/or situations. I prefer neither/nor—that is what the black-and-white paintings taught me. I found that there was a third entity out there: not black, not white, but existing over there in those greys."[8]

Rho is the seventeenth letter in the Greek alphabet. The painting is complex. It is present in its scale. It makes present what one is meant to feel or experience in relation to the painting in terms of planar light—the process of lighting a large surface—and texture. The painting, or what Whitten refers to as the "plane," is created in one gesture. As a Studio Museum in Harlem text observes:

> For the works in his "Greek Alphabet" series, Jack Whitten placed objects such as cords or wires on a hard surface and set a large canvas over them. He applied layers of gesso, pigment, and acrylic slip to the canvas, which he then raked with tools he called "developers," made from altered rakes, saws, and Afro combs. For the artist, these objects were symbolic of African-American identity and history. Whitten referred to this technique, which created a striated surface that appears lit from within, as "weaving light."[9]

Naming his tools "'processors' or 'developers,' in part in reference to photo-processing . . . [was] a measure of the way he was attempting to re-conceive the conceptual basis of his painting."[10] "Developer," in fact, makes explicit a connection to photography—and to processing. With it, Whitten found not just a mode of working, but a philosophy. "I

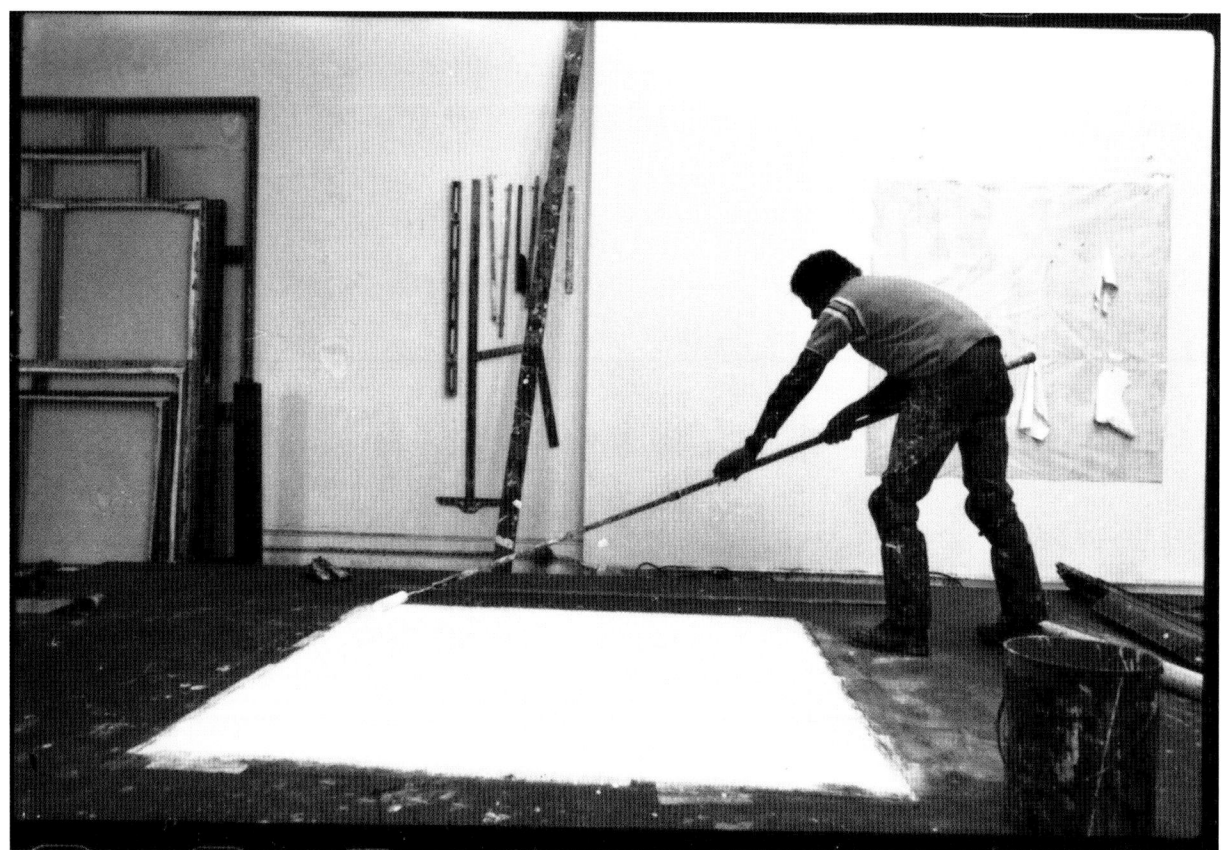

FIGURE 4
Jack Whitten working in his studio in the 1970s. Personal photo. © Jack Whitten Estate. Courtesy the Estate and Hauser & Wirth.

must learn to accept change as being inherent with my type of structure it is not a cookie cutter concept. One must allow for change—however rapid: as long as it is within the original boundaries."[11] He recalled that he "wanted a painting to exist as a single line. One gesture. . . . I spent ten years working on that drawing board. Bent over. Stooped down. I can't do that no more."[12] This is a split-second process. Even if Whitten returned to the painting, the crux of the work had been made in a matter of seconds. In *Rho I*, the process invites the viewer to think about the line. To consider the scratch. And that viewing bears out a relation to photography via a relation to the Xerox machine and to televisual static.

For Whitten the studio was a lab, a place of innovation and experimentation, and the work was to try to get rid of the hand. With the developer, something happens, something is made in one big pull. These paintings were created on the floor, and in the process of moving the developer across the canvas, the works, in effect, became a (kind of) collage [fig. 4]. And with that invention Whitten transported to painting part of what he had learned from watching his mother work removing color, remaking and recycling old clothing into something new.

Some parts of *Rho I* look like weavings; they have the quality of a fabric of various shades, textures, weights, and densities woven together. There are two horizontal lines that run almost through the entire painting. They seem to mark it off into quadrants and to cut through a work that is already cut through with lines, with texture and drag. There are thicker and thinner bands of black and white, there is gray, there is rub, drip, smear, and break. There are horizontal, vertical, and diagonal lines, clusters of markings, something that looks like a letter. The painting's surface gives way to the impression of depth and density. The marks evoke the surface and dimensionality of a washboard, as well as electricity, static, ghosted figures, and cartography. The objects that Whitten placed beneath the canvas before he dragged the developer across it became part of the frottage, a process of layering. That some of the objects are particular to Black life makes it one mode of visualizing—of mattering—Blackness in abstraction. It is an experiment in removing the hand and gesture from painting and in what happens when things, objects, rub together.

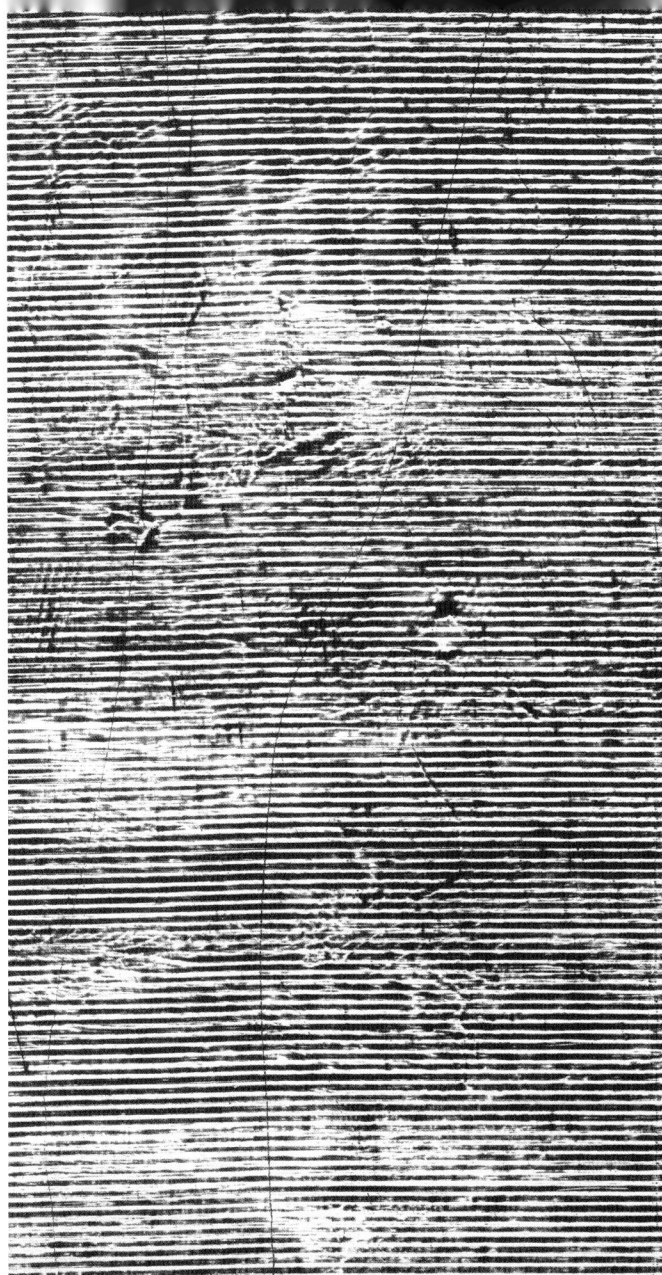
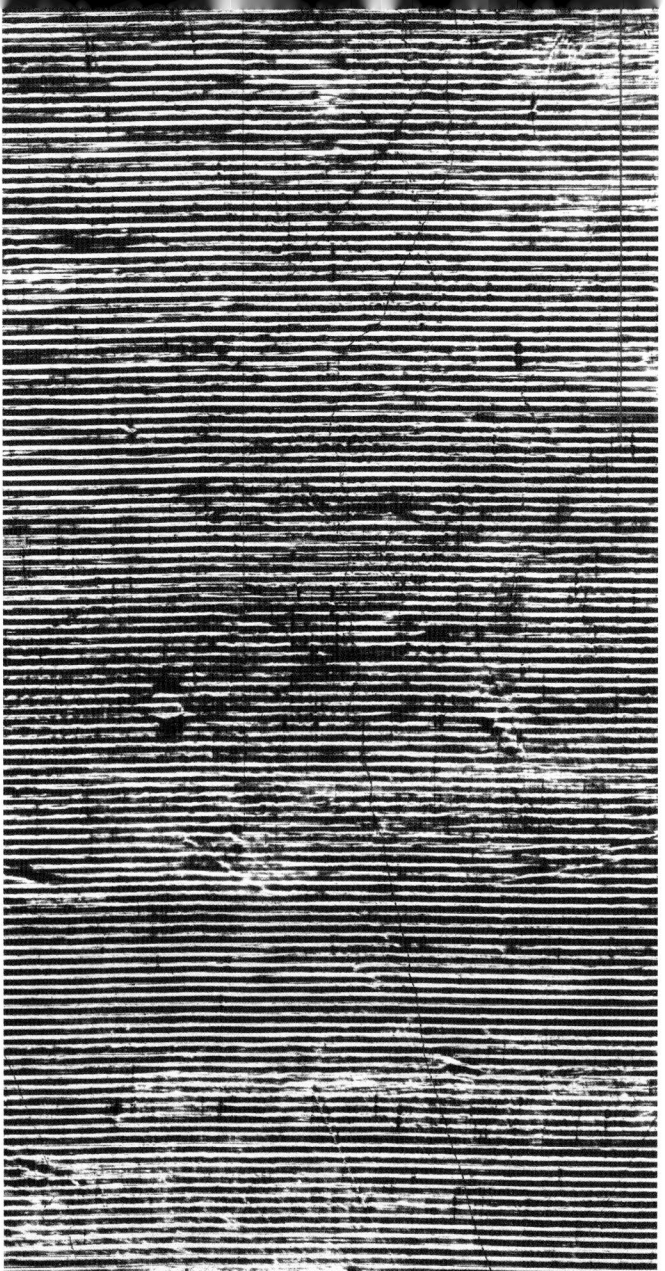

FIGURE 5a, b
Rho I (details), 1977. Jack Whitten. © Jack Whitten Estate. Courtesy the Estate and Hauser & Wirth.

On the surface of the painting [fig. 5a], its "highly structured skin,"[13] we see what has been described as shimmer.[14] Whitten said: "My interest is always how I can . . . direct the light." And light does seem to emerge from the painting's lines and striations, from within its very texture. The painting's illusion of radiance and shimmer directs the eye, recalling the atmospheric effects of different temperatures in its layering. This is perceptual drift.

Rho I and each of Whitten's Greek Alphabet paintings are synesthetic experiences. That this is so became even clearer to me when I watched a conversation between the poet, scholar, and writer Fred Moten and the composer and pianist Vijay Iyer, in which Moten turns his attention to those paintings. Moten speaks of how the works are striated [fig. 5b] and says that "they look like scores and looms." Staying with Moten's words, I too encounter in these paintings a sense of musicality and musical notation in which the vertical lines indicate arrangement. I also see the loom, the structure on which a weaving is made. Iyer's *Sensorium* is dedicated to Whitten, and running through all of Whitten's work is a deep connection to music—in fact, he once "described himself . . . as 'a quantum expressionist.'"[15] Whitten derived much inspiration for his work from jazz, and spoke of translating Coltrane's sheets of sound into sheets of light.[16] He once wrote: "I am a Jazzman. I adhere to Jazz as a Philosophy. The expansion of freedom is the philosophy of Jazz."[17]

Thinking about freedom, we might see in *Rho I*'s scoring a meeting with Charles Gaines's gridworks and *Manifestos* series, in which he "translate[s] the language of four political manifestos into musical scores accompanied by video."[18] Gaines's works—such as *Princes and Powers (After Baldwin)* (2018), *Malcolm X Speech at Ford Auditorium (1968)* (2013), and *Manifestos* (2008) [fig. 6]—are composed from a range of historical and political documents. Gaines says: "My work is about combining things or making relationships between things that are completely unrelated. In this case, the combination, of course, is the political manifestos and the music that is produced by them."[19] But these works produce their own music—they are notes that have reverberated and echoed. In Whitten's work we encounter the score in its other meanings as well, as in a cut or mark made with incisions.

In *A Black Gaze: Artists Changing How We See*, Tina Campt writes about perspective, feeling, and sitting on the floor of a gallery and looking (up) at works of art. "Writing to artwork from the floor of a gallery (or, in this case, an artist's studio) minimizes you as a viewer and maximizes the work itself. Looking up at it both breaks up and breaks down some of the traditional dynamics of spectatorship and visual mastery. And when the subject of that art is Black folks, challenging the dynamics of spectatorship and visual mastery is an extremely important intervention."[20]

To be in relation to Whitten's gridworks is to encounter what Chanda Laine Carey identifies as the "'geometric spectral,' an optical state where the painter has created a simultaneous sense of rich texture and smoothness that has intense effects on perception. A camera cannot capture such effects. Sgraffito enhances the surfaces of this series, where lines frequently move across planes bisected by semicircles."[21] That geometric spectral points to painters like Romare Bearden and Jacob Lawrence, who use the figure as well. Likewise, that line.

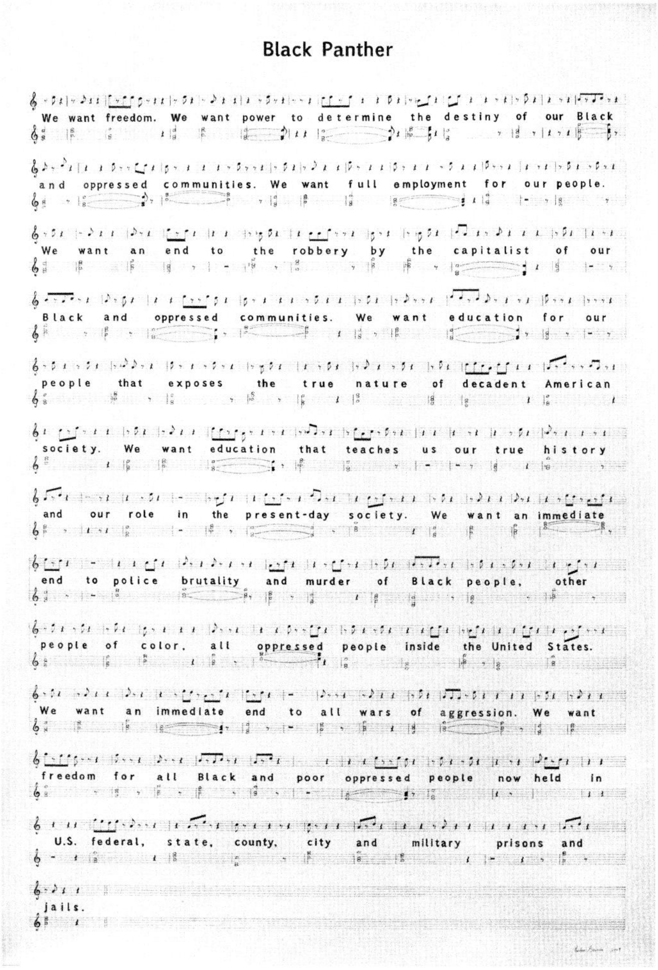

FIGURE 6
Manifestos (detail), 2008. Charles Gaines (American, born 1944). Four-channel black-and-white video installation with sound, four graphite drawings on paper, four monitors, four pedestals, two speakers; installation dimensions variable. © Charles Gaines. Courtesy the artist and Hauser & Wirth.

III. A "RESTLESS INGENUITY"[22]

For me abstraction is essence. What we do in abstraction is we take the whole of life and we distill it.—Jack Whitten[23]

Whitten was working out what an artist's relationship to material might be when, as in his own life, one's first materials came from skins that one had cured and dried. What might this relationship be and do when the materials and shapes come from a segregated and still rich childhood and young adulthood? The materials and shapes that Whitten engaged are the matter of life, of Black life in particular—in terms of aspect, sound, light, and feeling. Whitten worked and reworked these materials, observing that "painting is a continuous process"[24] . . . like a life.

In an interview with Hilarie M. Sheets in 2014, the artist Howardena Pindell recounted a formative moment that was part of what constituted her life in relation to the unconscious and the shapes of segregation. Of a series of 1977 paintings that make extensive use of the circle, including *Untitled #20: Dutch Wives, Circled and Squared* (1978) and *Untitled #18* (1977), Pindell said that when she started on those works her conscious intention was to explore the aesthetic possibilities of the circle. And then she began the work and was startled by the memory of a childhood experience. Born and raised in Philadelphia, Pindell was on a car ride with her father through Kentucky in the 1950s when they stopped at a root-beer stand and were served with mugs that had red circles placed on the bottom. "'I asked my father, "What is this red circle?"' she recalls. 'He said, "That's because we're black and we cannot use the same utensils as the whites." I realized that's really the origin of my being driven to try to change the circle in my mind, trying to take the sting out of that.'"[25] The circle was the mark by which segregation was enacted and maintained. To be outside of whiteness was to know, intimately, this particular circle's sting. In Pindell's work it is also the mark by which segregation's psychic and material hold might be unmade. The circle, a symbol of infinitude that has been mobilized by white supremacy for enclosure and restriction, arrests Pindell in a practice of restoring its larger generative properties. In other words, the circle confines, and it can also expand. Pindell has revealed that she was trying to undo the mark that the circle made in her mind and thereby also the mark it made out in the world. She was making

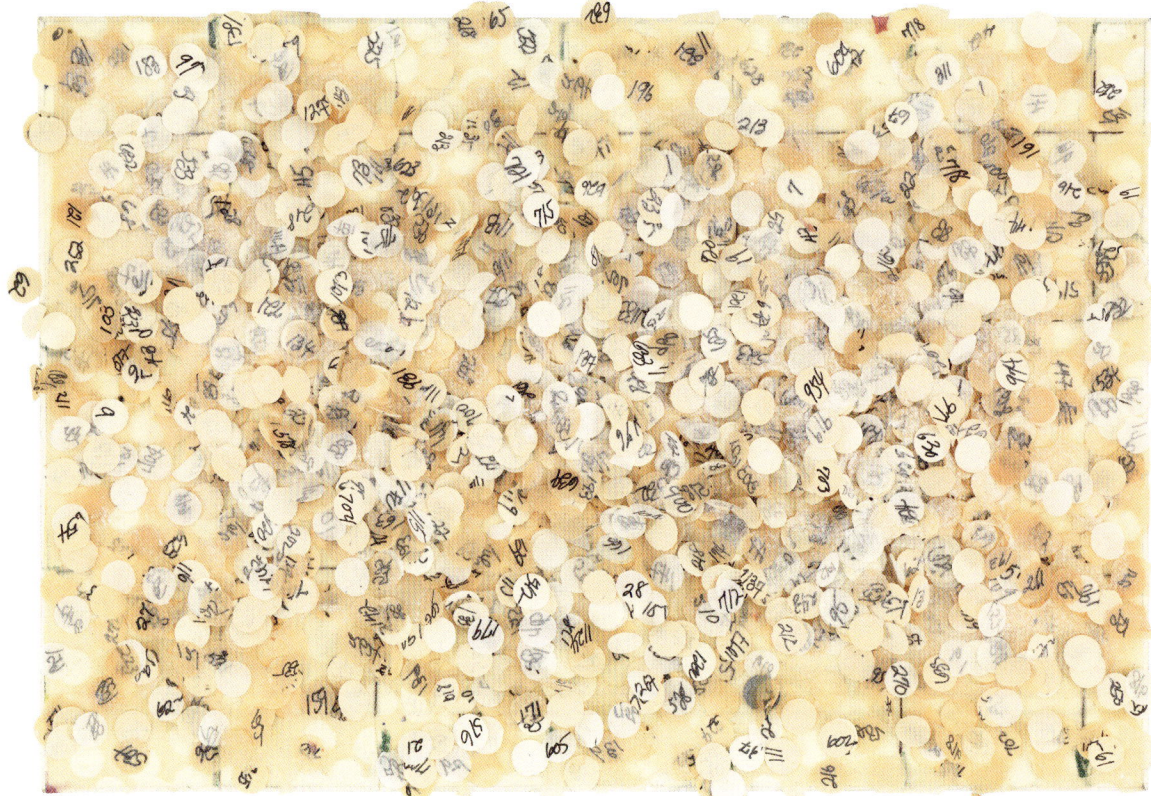

a new grammar, constructing new significatory possibilities. "I see that as the reason I have been obsessed with the circle . . . using it in a way that would be positive instead of negative."[26]

In Pindell's work circles multiply; in infinitesimal occurrences, the circle appears performing mathematical calculations and elegant mysteries. In *Untitled #58* (1974) [fig. 7], for example, circles carry numbers, some of whose significance may be known to Pindell, whose father was a mathematician; others, perhaps, are mysterious to the artist, and many are both mysterious and known by, which is to say of some significance to, the painting's viewers. Those circles are a kind of clerical confetti known as accounts, page numbers, and details, but they are also memory lists and other multitudinous somethings. Likewise, in Pindell's *Night Flight* (2015–16) [fig. 8] one has the sense of a blue baked earth above which one sees the complicated and shimmering equations of the life below and gleans a sense of the clarity and rapture of the light and constellations above. She is, she says, "at the stage where I want a sense of going outside the picture plane."[27] Pindell wants to add another kind of depth—to suture different worlds.

This suturing of worlds and movement outside of the picture plane brings me back to Whitten, who over the course of his life and career kept a journal that he referred to as "the woodshed," a term for rehearsal and exploration that comes from the jazz musicians with whom Whitten was in constant conversation. The journals are clarifying. In them are over fifty-five years of talks, notes, working entries, studio logs, and more, collected and published as *Jack Whitten: Notes from the Woodshed* (2018). They are the writings of an artist who from the beginning was questioning what his work might be, could be, could do. "I am an artist," he writes, "and my job is to decode the full spectrum of being human. The studio is a necessary sanctuary, a place of quiet and contemplation that allows me to do my work as a painter. My difficulty has always been one of faith: what justifies staying in the studio when the outside world is constantly testing my belief in art?"[28] In *Notes from the Woodshed*'s pages we meet an artist who is stretching the dimensions of what painting and sculpture and materials are and what they can do in the world.

In an entry dated May 17, 1974, Whitten details, in shorthand, his experimentation with materials and process. He has been using toner from Eastman Kodak and he finds that this is revolutionizing his process. "I tried the toner from Xerox, executed 12 drawings.

FIGURE 7
Untitled #58, 1974.
Howardena Pindell
(American, born 1943).
Mixed media on board;
12.7 x 20.3 cm. Collection
of James Keith Brown and
Eric Diefenbach, New York.
© Howardena Pindell.
Courtesy the artist and
Garth Greenan Gallery,
New York.

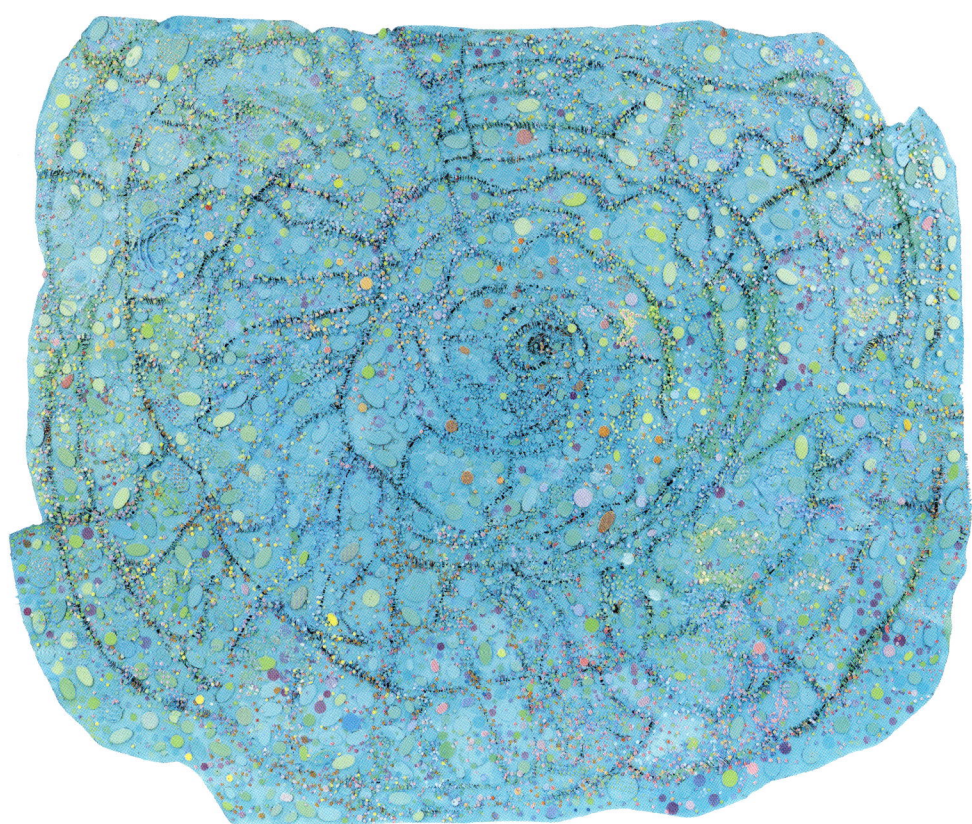

It worked just as I expected it to—IMMEDIATE—NATURAL—SPONEITY—VERY CRISP—EVERYTHING I'VE ALWAYS WANTED FROM A DRAWING—THANKS TO XEROX!"[29] This entry also includes his desire to show these paintings and raise cash, along with the financial details of his preparations to go to Crete for the summer. The entry concludes:

> I am on my way to glory
>
>   a child of the plane
>
>   the square is my play box
>
>   the triangle my source
>
>   the circle my absolute
>
> I am on my way to glory
>
> I am on my way to glory
>
> I am on my way to glory
>
> A Child of the plane.[30]

These jubilant verses take the form of a gospel song. But instead of glory being in heaven it is in the propulsive sense of innovation, exploration, and expansion of the relation between a plane, a square, a triangle, and a circle, each with its use and purpose (source, play box, absolute) on the way to glory. In this song of ambition Whitten declares himself a child of the plane, in the second instance with an uppercase *C*. The thrice repeated refrain "I am on my way to glory" uses the language and pacing of a spiritual; it is a joyous touchstone that marks a new method of painting for Whitten. This plane is not the picture plane as he has been taught—but rather one that perhaps he would later describe as a mapping of the soul.

Indeed, what Whitten presents here is a new cosmology, a different orientation and relation to space and material and axis, to gesture and history. This vocabulary of painting (the plane, the square, the triangle as "source,"[31] the box, the circle that is absolute) may be one that is shared, but the tense and the grammar diverge.[32] There is the practice,

FIGURE 8
Night Flight, 2015–16. Howardena Pindell. Mixed media on canvas; 190.5 x 160 cm. Collection of Philip Holzer, Frankfurt am Main. © Howardena Pindell. Courtesy the artist and Garth Greenan Gallery, New York.

and there is a decision to inhabit the radical present in which both history and material are pinned to the wall. "Formalism," Whitten wrote, "for me is a step toward something. It's a means—and that is all it is.[33]"

In this step toward a critical vocabulary of which the square, the triangle, the plane, and the circle are a part, a question is or might be: what additional weight do these ordinary shapes and tools bear when the artist who uses them has grown up in a world in which their own survival, their own bodily integrity, might depend on knowing which plane was theirs to enter, which square mile or stretch of land or water was off limits to them, how the circle marked the circumference, the diameter, and the radius of what was usable? When survival might depend on knowing the length of the line, or the circumscription of the grid, of knowing what was permissible for them. When survival might depend on another kind of understanding of the picture plane, one in which the individual or the community internalizes a map, imbibes an intimate knowledge of where one is positioned in the space, the geography, of the plane.

Let us return to that op-ed by Whitten published in the Walker Art Center's online magazine *Sightlines* in 2015, in which the artist takes a measure of this kind of knowing and of making art in times of unremitting violence. He recounts a particular instance of childhood ingenuity and play that was both constituted counter to white supremacy and anti-Blackness and then interdicted by them:

> Summertime in Bessemer, Alabama, is hot, sticky, and muggy. Growing up there, it was forbidden for Black kids to swim in the local city pool, which was reserved for Whites only. The older boys in our community built a dam of mud, tree branches, and stones on Parson's Creek. The dam made a perfect swimming hole. We even tied a car tire with a rope to an overhead tree limb, which allowed us to swing into the water. It was great fun! One morning our fun ended abruptly after the first kid to jump into the swimming hole came out screaming with bloody feet. Evidently the white people thought that the Niggers were having too much fun and under the cover of darkness threw bushels of broken glass bottles into our swimming hole.[34]

In the language of landscape architecture, the circle is the mark made for a tree. There are multiple circles in Whitten's narration. There is the circle that marks the zone of exclusion wherein Black children are prohibited from swimming in the city pool. There is the circle of community in which Black boys, older and younger, together come up with and execute a plan to solve their exclusion from the pleasures of swimming and diving in the heat and humidity of an Alabama summer. Within this circle, they construct a dam and a swimming hole, and they secure a rope and a tire. There is the circle of the car tire and the loop of the rope that attaches it to the tree limb. These circles are the means by which the boys suspended themselves, soared into the air, and launched themselves into the cool water.

In 2019, at Columbia University Graduate School of Architecture, Planning, and Preservation (GSAPP), the architect Mabel O. Wilson and the painter and sculptor Torkwase Dyson had a conversation about abstraction, its many languages, and its relationship to Black life. For Dyson, the possibilities, that rich stuff afforded by Black abstraction, are not unlike the dried animal skin that Whitten and his friends experimented with. This is the work of Black Compositional Thought, Dyson's ongoing theorization of Black life, defined in the introduction to the booklet accompanying her GSAPP exhibition *1919: Blackwater* as "a working term that considers how spatial networks—paths, throughways, water, architecture, and geographies—are composed by black bodies and how the attendant properties of energy, space, and objects interact as networks of liberation."[35] That dried skin of Whitten's was an object that they used counter to the ways (practical or otherwise) that others imagined for it. It became for Whitten a surface for re-imagining and re-visioning the world. Whitten made visual vocabularies that did what he needed them to do; he worked the forms of abstract expressionism.

I have returned repeatedly to Whitten's and Dyson's respective practices and imaginings. Specifically, I've been thinking with and about their relationships to materials. In that conversation with Wilson, Dyson extrapolated on Black invention and freedom

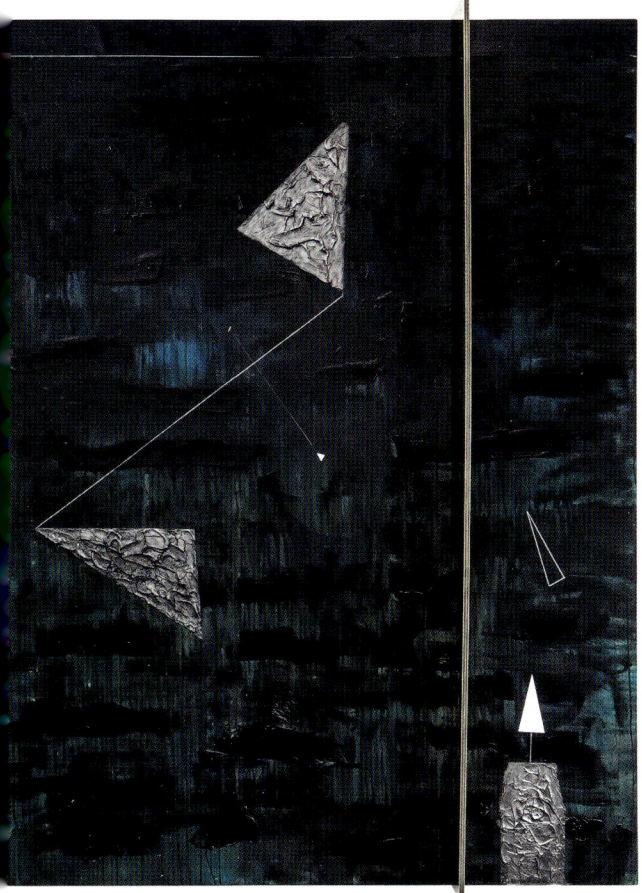
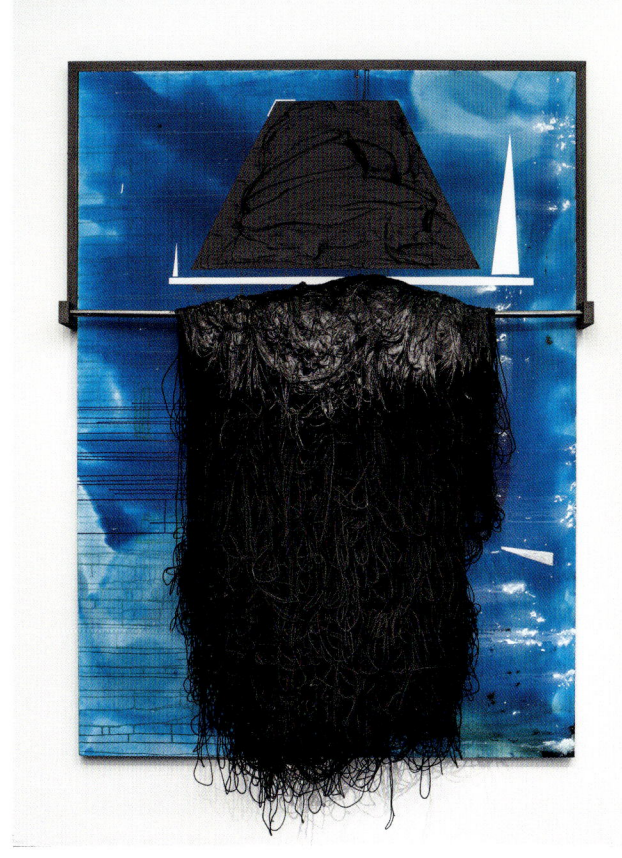

FIGURE 9
Hot Cold (Black Water 1919), 2019. Torkwase Dyson. Acrylic, graphite, string, wood, brass, and ink on canvas; 243.8 x 182.9 cm. © Torkwase Dyson, courtesy Pace Gallery. Photo: Nicholas Knight.

FIGURE 10
Pilot, 2019. Torkwase Dyson (American, born 1973). Acrylic, graphite, string, wood, ink on canvas; 243.8 x 182.9 cm. © Torkwase Dyson, courtesy Pace Gallery. Photo: Nicholas Knight.

drives; she was thinking about seventeen-year-old Eugene Williams and the raft that he and many other boys made in the summer of 1919. The introduction to the exhibition booklet tells us that "the story of Eugene Williams offers Dyson a historical framework to think through the relationship between race, climate migration, and the architectural imagination."[36]

For Dyson, the teenage boys' handmade raft showed their intimate and detailed knowledge of which neighborhoods to skirt (grids and topography) and what pockets of water to avoid (depth and flow) as they made their way to and then down Lake Michigan. Each part of their plan displayed Black Compositional Thinking. And Dyson centers their tremendous imaginations, and their radical ingenuity, in the face of segregation [figs. 9, 10]. As William Tuttle Jr.'s essay in the exhibition booklet describes:

The product of several weeks of work by a dozen-and-a-half teenagers, the raft was "a tremendous thing," fully fourteen by nine feet, with a "big chain with a hook on one of the big logs, and we'd put a rope through it and tie it." Harris [one of the boys who made the raft] and his friends were far from being expert swimmers, but they could hang onto the raft and propel it forward by kicking; and, occasionally, "we could swim under water and dive under water and come up," always making sure, however, that they were within easy distance of the raft. "As long as the raft was there," Harris noted, "we were safe."[37]

In Whitten's "A Circle of Blood" he demonstrated, again, this thinking, this making, this navigating of a hostile world through the terrain of material and imagination. When I look at *Rho I*'s horizontal and vertical lines, its sandblasted quality, I see woodgrain and I imagine that painting laid out as a raft—a made object that indexes Whitten's innovation and desire for artistic freedom just as the boys' raft and dammed swimming hole manifested theirs. Each measured the longitude and the latitude, the depth and density of those waters, that air, those deeply and violently segregated spaces.

Both Whitten and Pindell have been subject to criticism for their uses of abstraction; they have been criticized for the forms they use. But as Saul Ostrow has observed, "focusing on form was a means of absorbing and coping with the political and social tensions of the '60s and '70s, even as this pursuit was viewed by some as being inherently Eurocentric and formalist, and its black practitioners in denial of their identity and responsibilities."[38] Indeed, Whitten made the forms he needed in order to do the work that he needed to do, because for him theory and material are the same thing. This strategy is, I think, analogous to that of Dyson, who has said: "I make spatial systems that build upon the architectural typologies that people have used to liberate themselves. These systems also consider infrastructure and the environment to create a visual amalgamation that recognizes the ways that black people move through, inhabit, cleave and form space."[39]

IV. IN RELATION

I discovered that embedded in the geometric construct of African sculpture is a three-dimensional grid which contains the DNA of visual perception.
—Jack Whitten[40]

Whitten is part of a constellation of Black artists who work not only in the languages of something called Abstract Expressionism but also in its black matter. Among his contemporaries were Alma Thomas, Sam Gilliam, Howardena Pindell, Lorraine O'Grady, Frank Bowling, Norm Lewis, Romare Bearden, Melvin Edwards, Charles Gaines, Jacob Lawrence, Betty Blayton, Mildred Thompson, Edward Clark, and then Nick Cave, Leonardo Drew, Torkwase Dyson, Dawoud Bey, Nari Ward, Adam Pendleton, and many others.

In 2018 there was a large show of Whitten's sculptures at the Met Breuer. This was the first time that these works he had been making in the summers for almost sixty years were shown. Summers were devoted to his sculptures. A number of critics who write about them read them through a split or bifurcation—there were the paintings that he continued to make and show and that were circulated in "art markets" and the sculptures that he made in summers, first in upstate New York and then in Crete, which went unexhibited. In each form, Whitten engaged a set of concerns and ideas (around material and spirit) on different planes. There is the horizontal picture plane and then, also, the vertical tree.

In the first entry in *Notes from the Woodshed*, Whitten writes: "Jacob Lawrence opened at the Whitney last night. It was a mob—a fantastic black swarm of people in color reaping the harvest of a hero."[41] When Whitten spoke of many of his years in New York,

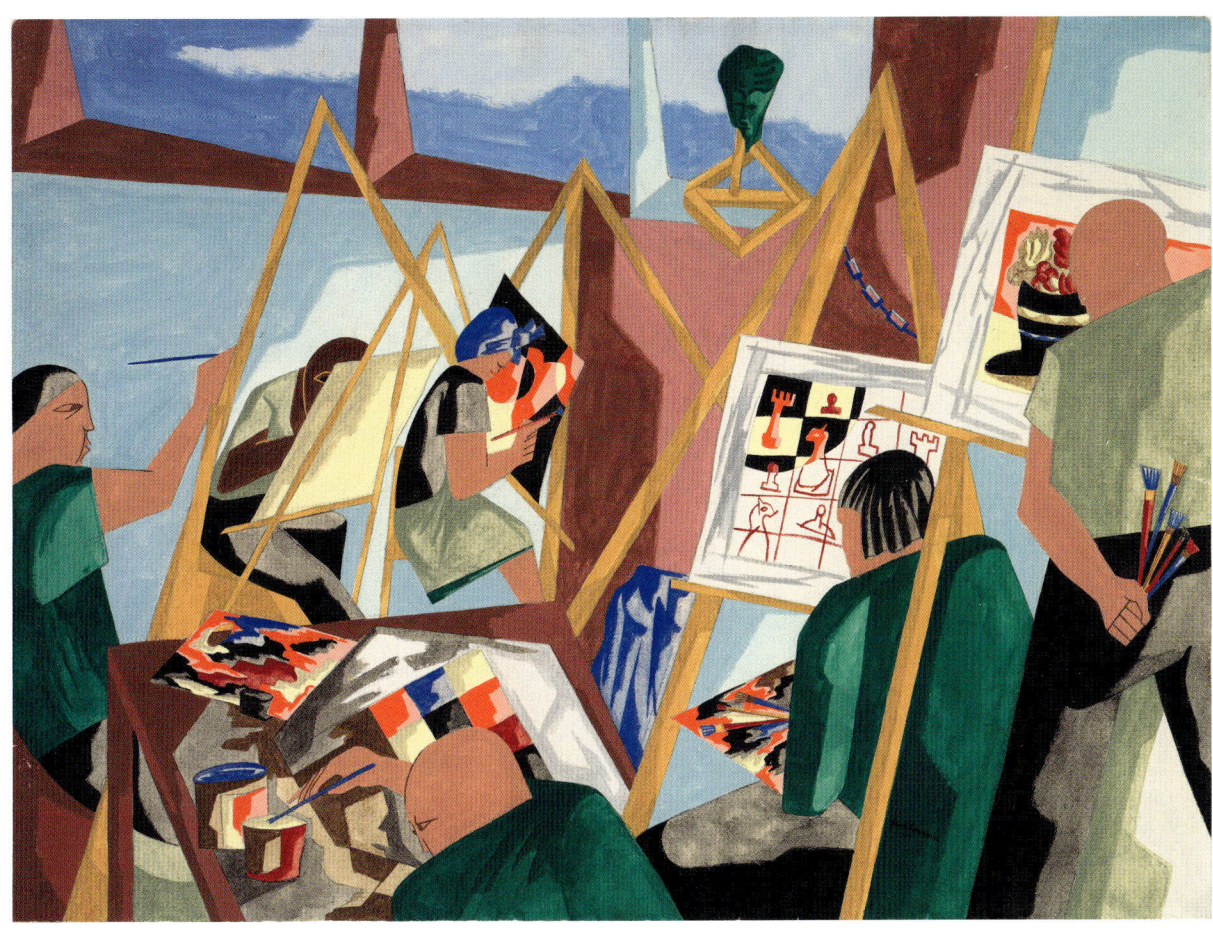

FIGURE 11
Creative Therapy, 1949. Jacob Lawrence (American, 1917–2000). Casein over graphite; 56 x 76.4 cm. The Cleveland Museum of Art, Delia E. Holden Fund, 1994.2. © 2022 The Jacob and Gwendolyn Knight Lawrence Foundation, Seattle / Artist Rights Society (ARS), New York.

the work he was making, his influences and comrades, Lawrence was always there. As was Bearden, whom he credited with giving him the confidence to be an artist. And he returned often to Lawrence on plasticity, remembering being advised by him to "keep it plastic man, maintain the structure." Whitten recalled a dream he'd had when he was preparing to go to Crete: "Two nights before leaving, I had this amazing dream of a tree standing in a clearing. The limbs were cut off, pruned, and the dream was a command: *When you go to Greece you are to find this tree and carve it into a totem.* It freaked me out, to say the least. I've always carved wood in the summer months; before we started going to Greece I worked upstate in the summers."[42] Whitten finds the tree, carves it, and that place becomes their summer home. Whitten was a visionary. With the sculptures Whitten follows Lawrence's advice and keeps it plastic.

That advice speaks to agility, practice, form, and dedication. Collected along with *Rho I* at the Cleveland Museum of Art is Lawrence's *Creative Therapy* (1949) [fig. 11], one of a series of eleven paintings the artist made while he was in the psychiatric ward of Hillside Hospital in Queens, where he spent over a year.[43] Lawrence's work returns me to Whitten and to his thinking about, his insistence on, what art does—what the practice and process of painting made possible for him and what it kept intact. It returns me to the plane of light, of thought and feeling. Indeed, in this painting and in much of Lawrence's abstract and figurative work from this period, planar light and angularity, tension, fatigue, and sometimes jubilation or quietude are so present—narratively and also in the way that he uses paint and light.

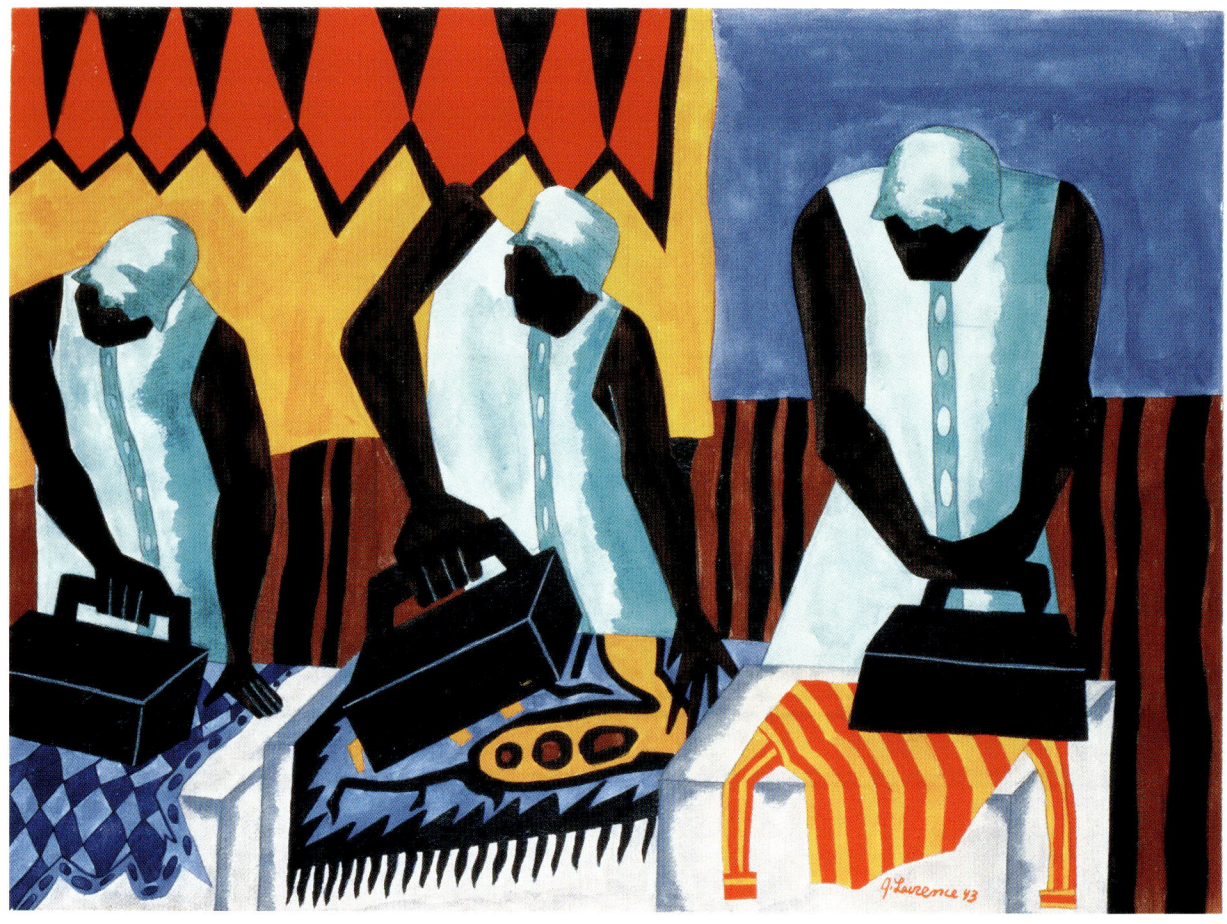

FIGURE 12
Ironers, 1943. Jacob Lawrence. Gouache on paper; 54.6 x 74.9 cm. Private collection. © 2022 The Jacob and Gwendolyn Knight Lawrence Foundation, Seattle / Artist Rights Society (ARS), New York. Photo: The Jacob and Gwendolyn Lawrence Foundation / Art Resource, New York.

One thinks, as well, of Lawrence's Panel 57 from the *Migration Series: The female workers were the last to arrive north*, or a work like his *Ironers* (1943) [fig. 12], its colors and lines, the lifted shoulders and the concentration of the three women dressed in white whose job it is to repeatedly use those heavy irons in order to press clothing or other materials—one sees the labor in them, in the planes.

Though there are figures in some of his earliest work, it is not the figure in Lawrence's work that finds itself in Whitten's; rather, they share concerns that the light, the line, and the paint make palpable. This is, as Whitten might say, art as a counter to evil. As he once explained:

> I use the word *antidote*. There is so much shit going on in society that I don't believe in—the only thing I believe in is *art*. I have nothing else. Art is the only thing I've got to go on, and I see it as being able to provide an antidote to all this evil shit that is going on. And it is *evil*—I cannot stress that enough. Obviously, it's going to get much worse too. We haven't seen nothing yet. All of us will be tested—that I can promise you.[44]

Whitten practiced new modes and ways of seeing, new methods of apprehending scale and light [fig. 13]. He gifted us with languages of sense and world making, what Dyson has called "a new kind of visual thinking"[45] in the midst of catastrophe. Art as a necessary way to alter and heighten perception. Art as antidote to violence.

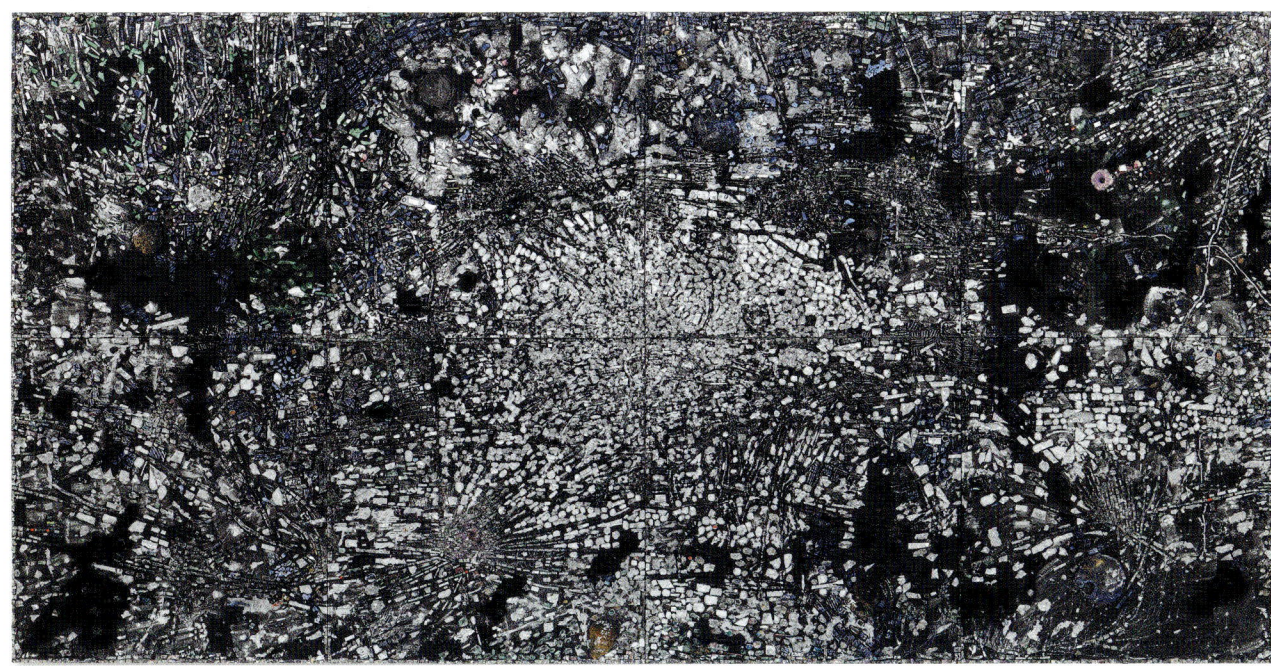

FIGURE 13
Atopolis: For Édouard Glissant, 2014. Jack Whitten. Acrylic on canvas, 8 panels; overall: 316.2 x 631.2 cm. The Museum of Modern Art, New York, Acquired through the generosity of Sid R. Bass, Lonti Ebers, Agnes Gund, Henry and Marie-Josée Kravis, Jerry Speyer and Katherine Farley, and Daniel and Brett Sundheim, 271.2017.a–h. © Jack Whitten Estate. Courtesy the Estate and Hauser & Wirth. Digital Image © The Museum of Modern Art / Licensed by SCALA / Art Resource, New York.

The quotation in this essay's title is from Jack Whitten, "A Circle of Blood: Jack Whitten on Art in Times of Unspeakable Violence," *Sightlines* (Walker Art Center), December 3, 2015, https://walkerart.org/magazine/jack-whitten-art-violence.

1. Jack Whitten in "The Art of Jack Whitten," interview with Stuart Horodner, Atlanta, May 15, 2008, Forum Network, https://forum-network.org/lectures/the-art-jack-whitten/.

2. Ibid.

3. Jack Whitten in "Jack Whitten: 'The political is in the work,'" TateShots artist video, October 31, 2017, https://www.tate.org.uk/art/videos/tateshots/jack-whitten-political-work.

4. Marc Godfrey and Allie Biswas, eds. *The Soul of a Nation Reader: Writings by and about Black American Artists, 1960–1980* (New York: Gregory R. Miller & Co., 2021), 32–33.

5. Kenneth Goldsmith, "Jack Whitten by Kenneth Goldsmith," *BOMB* 48, July 1, 1984, https://bombmagazine.org/articles/jack-whitten/.

6. Alex Greenberger, "An Old-School Painter Adapts to a New World Order: Jack Whitten's 50-Year Evolution," *Artnews*, January 19, 2016, https://www.artnews.com/art-news/artists/an-old-school-painter-adapts-to-a-new-world-order-jack-whittens-fifty-year-evolution-5632/.

7. Whitten, "The Art of Jack Whitten."

8. Jack Whitten in "In Conversation: Jack Whitten with Jarrett Earnest," *The Brooklyn Rail*, February 2017, https://brooklynrail.org/2017/02/art/JACK-WHITTEN-with-Jarrett-Earnest.

9. "Jack Whitten, *Khee I*, 1978," The Studio Museum in Harlem, accessed January 9, 2022, https://studiomuseum.org/collection-item/khee-i.

10. "Jack Whitten, *Epsilon Group II*, 1977," Tate, accessed January 21, 2022, https://www.tate.org.uk/art/artworks/whitten-epsilon-group-ii-t13803.

11. Colony Little, "'I Am Black, Angry, Tired of Teaching, Tired of Being Poor': Jack Whitten's Newly Published Journals Reveal a Long, Painful Road to Recognition," *Artnet*, August 6, 2018, https://news.artnet.com/art-world/jack-whittens-newly-published-journals-1327919.

12. Jack Whitten in "Jack Whitten: An Artist's Life," Art21 "Extended Play," March 21, 2018, https://www.youtube.com/watch?v=GFVsd450nCU.

13. Jack Whitten in *Jack Whitten: Notes from the Woodshed*, ed. Katy Siegel (New York: Hauser & Wirth, 2018), 117.

14. Saul Ostrow has written of *Rho I* that "as light rakes across the finely ridged surface, the paint shimmers." See Ostrow, "From the Archives: Process, Image and Elegy," *Art in America*, April 1, 2008, https://www.artnews.com/art-in-america/features/archives-process-image-elegy-2-63548/.

15. Jack Whitten, quoted in Bella Gould, "New Vijay Iyer and Craig Taborn Release, The Transitory Poems, Due March 15 on ECM," February 6, 2019, Music Works International, https://www.musicworksinternational.com/new-vijay-iyer-and-craig-taborn-release-the-transitory-poems-due-march-15-on-ecm/.

16. See "Vijay Iyer and Craig Taborn, The Transitory Poems," *Roulette*, March 12, 2019, https://roulette.org/event/vijay-iyer-and-craig-taborn-the-transitory-poems/.

17. Whitten, *Notes from the Woodshed*, 304.

18. "Charles Gaines: *Manifestos* Screening and Q&A," Hammer Museum, Los Angeles, June 17, 2020, https://hammer.ucla.edu/programs-events/2020/online-charles-gaines-manifestos-screening.

19. "Charles Gaines, *Manifestos 2*, 2013," Museum of Modern Art, New York, accessed January 9, 2022, https://www.moma.org/audio/playlist/272/3536. See also A. Will Brown, "Charles Gaines: 'I am dealing in the area of how meaning is formed,'" *Studio International*, October 8, 2015, https://www.studiointernational.com/index.php/charles-gaines-interview-i-am-dealing-in-the-area-of-how-meaning-is-formed.

20. Tina M. Campt, *A Black Gaze: Artists Changing How We See* (Cambridge, MA: MIT Press, 2021), 28.

21. Chanda Laine Carey, "Ars and Techne: Jack Whitten Retrospective," *Nka: Journal of Contemporary African Art* 40 (2017): 24.

22. This quote is taken from "In Conversation: Jack Whitten with Jarrett Earnest."

23. Whitten, in ibid.

24. Ibid.

25. Hilarie M. Sheets, "The Changing Complex Profile of Black Abstract Painters" (July 2014), excerpted in "From the Archives: Howardena Pindell's Rich Visual Feasts Throughout the Years," *Artnews*, January 26, 2018, https://www.artnews.com/art-news/retrospective/archives-howardena-pindells-rich-visual-feasts-throughout-years-9707/.

26. James Panero, "Seeing Her Worldview in a Circle," *Wall Street Journal*, September 1, 2018, https://www.wsj.com/articles/seeing-her-worldview-in-a-circle-1535799601.

27. Howardena Pindell in "Controlled Chaos: Howardena Pindell Interviewed by Jessica Lanay," *BOMB*, May 14, 2018, https://bombmagazine.org/articles/controlled-chaos-howardena-pindell-interviewed/.

28. Jack Whitten, "A Circle of Blood."

29. Whitten, *Notes from the Woodshed*, 78.

30. Ibid.

31. About the triangle, Whitten wrote, "When I speak of a geometrical figure I am speaking of a reduction of an African wood carving. My idea of a triangle is that figure which is arrived deducted from an African carving, the reduction of a square, or rectangle, or trapezoid. etc. These geometrical figures are the matter of African carving." See ibid., 121–22.

32. When one thinks of the square one might think as well of Kazimir Malevich's *Black Square* and recall that in 2015, researchers in Russia examined the

painting under a microscope and found a handwritten note that they believe reads: "Battle of negroes in a dark cave." They discovered a racist joke written on the canvas. See Carey Dunne, "Art Historians Find Racist Joke Hidden Under Malevich's 'Black Square,'" *Hyperallergic*, November 13, 2015, https://hyperallergic.com/253361/art-historian-finds-racist-joke-hidden-under-malevichs-black-square/.

33. Whitten, "In Conversation: Jack Whitten with Jarrett Earnest."

34. Whitten, "A Circle of Blood."

35. Introduction to "Torkwase Dyson, *1919: Black Water*," ed. Irene Sunwoo, exhibition booklet (New York: Arthur Ross Architecture Gallery, Columbia GSAPP, 2019), 15.

36. Ibid.

37. William Tuttle Jr., "The Red Summer and the Red Scare," in "Torkwase Dyson, *1919: Black Water*," 10.

38. Ostrow, "From the Archives: Process, Image, and Elegy."

39. Torkwase Dyson, quoted in "Torkwase Dyson, *1919: Black Water*," 4.

40. Jack Whitten, "June 4, 1984," in *The Soul of a Nation Reader*, 612.

41. Whitten, *Notes from the Woodshed*, 12.

42. Whitten, "In Conversation: Jack Whitten with Jarrett Earnest."

43. See "One-Way Ticket: Jacob Lawrence's Migration Series, 1949–50," Museum of Modern Art, New York, accessed January 9, 2022, https://www.moma.org/interactives/exhibitions/2015/onewayticket/jacob-lawrence/24/, and "Over the Line: The Art and Life of Jacob Lawrence," Whitney Museum of American Art, New York, accessed January 9, 2022, https://whitney.org/www/jacoblawrence/overview.html.

44. Whitten, "In Conversation: Jack Whitten with Jarrett Earnest."

45. Torkwase Dyson in "Torkwase Dyson in Conversation with Mabel O. Wilson: Black Compositional Thought," in "Torkwase Dyson, *1919: Black Water*," 16.

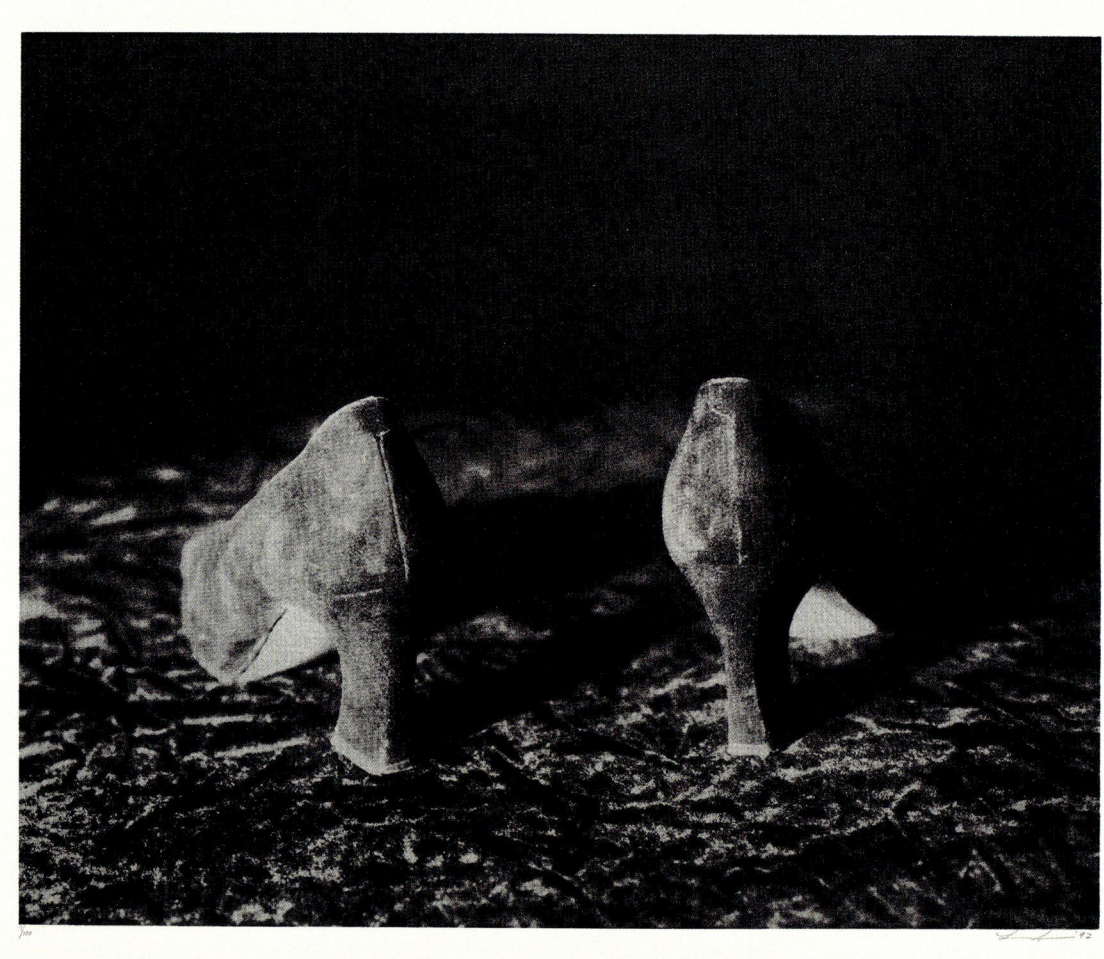

CURE / HEAL

LIBERATORY DISSEMBLANCE:
AN APPROACH TO LORNA SIMPSON'S *CURE/HEAL*
KEY JO LEE

Simpson resists what her viewers—all viewers—consider their authority: her work demands that we speculate, investigate. . . . What am I looking at and for? What am I projecting onto what's here? What must I let go of?
—Margo Jefferson[1]

But what of our own posture? What does it mean for us . . . to look at a row of women who will not look back?
—Huey Copeland[2]

Margo Jefferson's and Huey Copeland's insights set the stage for the kind of object oriented and self-investigatory analytic approach that *Cure/Heal* (1992) [fig. 14], and in fact Lorna Simpson's entire oeuvre, requires of its viewers.[3] A cultural critic and historian, Jefferson was led to this fluid and ever-reflexive set of queries by one of Simpson's ink and screenprint collages, such as *Back of Yellow Dress* [fig. 15] from her 2013 series *Ebony Collages*, which brings the viewer's intellectual and psychological desires into persistent consciousness. Copeland, an art historian and curator, draws the viewer's body into a burgeoning interpretive network by invoking our posture as he analyzes an image/text work from much earlier in Simpson's career, like *Guarded Conditions* from 1989 [fig. 16]. We often have high expectations for an artwork's expressiveness. We anticipate that the best art will reveal truth and provoke emotion, but we don't often consider what is required of us to perceive those revelations or to be receptive to both intellectual and emotional engagement. This essay seeks to demonstrate how the edicts of perceptual drift—intention, and slow and multisensory engagement, in this case with memory and materiality, overt self-consciousness, collaborative meaning-making, and disciplinary openness—might serve this deceptively simple black-and-white image by articulating the rewards of careful address. What will emerge is a constellation of artworks, artists, and historical moments as well as theoretical and pedagogical frameworks, ekphrastic descriptions, and personal asides, their linear and nonlinear connections revealing otherwise imperceptible histories and narratives and—all the while—generating new uncertainties, inspiring new inquiries, and articulating new connections. What follows is my attempt to narrate such an experience of perceptual drift activated by this single work of art.

Simpson's enigmatic screenprint *Cure/Heal*, while compositionally spare and modestly sized, offers an immodest sensory feast that is revealed only through deliberate attention. This rectangular black-and-white image is framed by a bone-colored border. Two suede pumps rest akimbo atop a sheet of crushed velvet, pointing away at opposite obliques with heels facing the viewer. There are no discernable logos or labels, and the toe boxes are hidden from view such that one could only guess at their shape. We recognize the materials—suede and velvet—through Simpson's use of light, which sweeps in from the left, dappling the crushed velvet beneath the shoes and illuminating each one's soles, seams, and shallow surface depressions. The light simultaneously emphasizes the shadows cast by each shoe, which cut sharply to the right, carving a purposeful sightline into the murky depths of a tenebrous background. The image, though materially rich, tells us little about the shoes. Centered below this tableau, two words, "Cure" and "Heal," hover in blood red against the pale border, asserting an immediate yet subtle tension between the work's two-dimensionality and its sensuousness. This, for me, is the first hint at its desire for complex engagement. At first witness, it drew me to reverie, and so it is here we begin.

FIGURE 14
10: The Artist as Catalyst: *Cure/Heal*, 1992. Lorna Simpson (American, born 1960). Screenprint; image: 40 x 50 cm. The Cleveland Museum of Art, Gift of Linda and Jack Lissauer, M.D., to commemorate The Print Club of Cleveland's centennial, 2019, 2019.73.4. © Lorna Simpson, courtesy the artist and Hauser & Wirth.

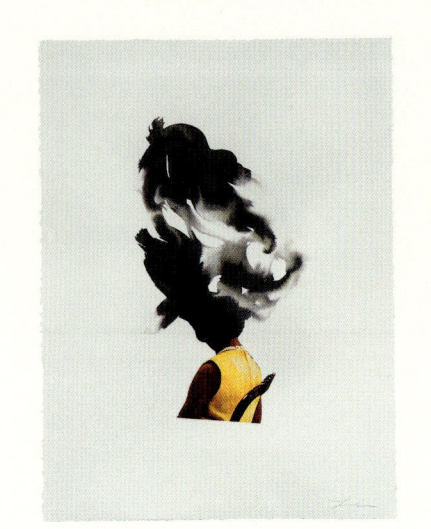
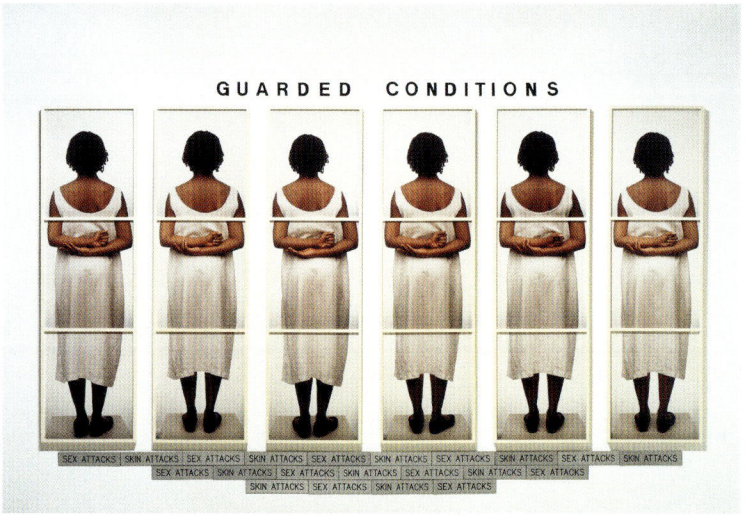

FIGURE 15
Back of Yellow Dress, 2013. Lorna Simpson. Collage and ink on paper; image: 74.9 x 54.9 cm. © Lorna Simpson, courtesy the artist and Hauser & Wirth.

FIGURE 16
Guarded Conditions, 1989. Lorna Simpson. 18 color Polaroid prints; 21 engraved plastic plaques, and 17 plastic letters; overall: 231.1 x 376.6 x 4.1 cm. Photo: Phillipp Scholz Rittermann. © Lorna Simpson, courtesy the artist and Hauser & Wirth.

    Ours isn't one of the Black families that have, or at least have held onto, an ancestral chronicle.[4] And even though present, my mother, grandmother, and great-aunts were as familiar and opaque in equal measure as these vacant, mid-heel pumps. The inky palette of the image, too, summons my mother's and grandmother's sable soft skin, complexions so deep and rich. I look like them both, but most startlingly like Theresa, my mother, who brought light and cast shadows unpredictably. Thus, Simpson's image immediately conjures three generations—my grandmother's, my mother's, and my own—and speaks to patterns of display and concealment I inherited in its bright and hushed tones.

    When I was nine, my grandmother took me to see the play *Mama, I Want to Sing!* at the Heckscher Theatre off-Broadway. We got dressed up, hair coiffed, dresses pressed, my grandma with her purse and always matching shoes, and drove from Newark into Manhattan. I was used to being surrounded by Black folks and therefore accustomed to the glow we exude, but the sea of people heading into that theater shone so bright as to be blinding. I was immediately hooked and asked when we could do it again. The answer was very soon, and the next show to which we ventured was *Dreamgirls*, that same year. If I thought the Heckscher Theatre was a gateway to Black brilliance, well, the Imperial Theatre on Broadway was the portal to Black nirvana. Never had I seen so many beautiful tawnies, cedars, and umbers bedecked in gorgeous, richly hued dresses (for it is the women that I remember most). Lips from cinnamon to cerise seemed to smile just at me. So I was already in love with everything before we even got to our seats. When the curtain call rang and the milling crowd became a throng, these sights became sounds as taffeta and silk, brocade and velvet, tweed and leather brushed against one another. These sounds gained sensuality as they surrounded and caressed me. From my low vantage, faces disappeared, hands and feet became the focus. Forty-four years hence, some details have receded; others are incredibly sharp. And when I close my eyes and dwell in that moment, just below the din of adult voices, what I hear most clearly is a chorus of click-clacks. The shoes.

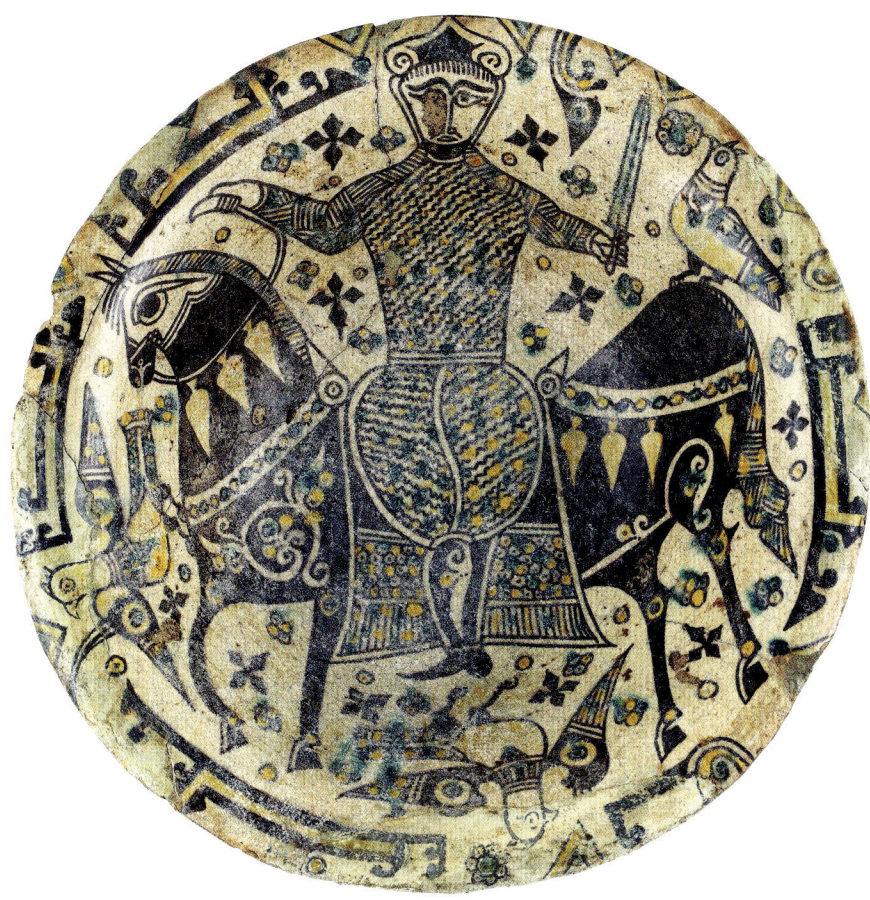

FIGURE 17
Dish with Rider, 800s or 900s. Neyshabur (Northeast Iran). Unknown artist. Earthenware, underglaze painting. h. 6 cm; diam. 22 cm. Museum für Islamische Kunst, Staatliche Museen, Berlin, Inv. I. 11/62. Photo: bpk Bildagentur / Museum für Islamische Kunst, Staatliche Museen, Berlin / Hans Kraeftner / Art Resource, New York.

THE LIBERATORY POTENTIAL OF VACANT SHOES

Fascinatingly, high-heeled shoes were first designed to ensure safety. For members of the tenth-century Persian cavalry, they were a means of keeping soldiers' feet firmly in stirrups, as shown on the *Dish with Rider* [fig. 17].[5] For several centuries high-heeled boots and shoes were considered emblems of masculinity and riding utility across Asia and the Near East, which may have been what influenced European men to take up the style in their riding attire by the turn of the seventeenth century. The association of masculinity with heels was so pervasive that an avant-garde of women who by the 1630s had taken to wearing them were deemed unflatteringly "mannish." The utilitarian origins of heels swiftly faded, and the shoes underwent an aesthetic transformation, going from expressing militarism and outdoorsy manliness—and a willful "mannishness" when worn by women—to serving as emblems of aristocratic elegance. Heels rose even higher toward the end of the seventeenth century, when King Louis XIV of France famously began wearing extraordinarily opulent clothing bedecked with trims like fur, feathers, and lace, as well as jewels, his red leather-wrapped stacked heels serving as a literal marker of his elevated political standing.[6] It's important to note that over the course of the seventeenth century, as "the type of heels on men's footwear expressed two distinctly different forms masculinity, the refined man of elegance and the man of action," women were also donning heels more and more.[7] Both men's and women's heels rose higher during this time. However, while men's square-toed stacked heels retained their sturdiness, stability, and relative comfort, the toe boxes and heels on women's shoes "tapered to increasingly narrow points."[8] There was a deep shift in men's fashion at the turn of the eighteenth century that saw few men continuing to wear high heels, as Enlightenment thought promoted universal rationality and the political enfranchisement of all European men, regardless of class, and simultaneously deemed women "naturally deficient in reason" and therefore not meant to hold political or economic power.[9] As men's feet became more grounded, women's bodies were precariously stilted. Heels, once meant to solve a military problem, were now used to highlight a woman's curves as an appeal to men—an idea that persists today.

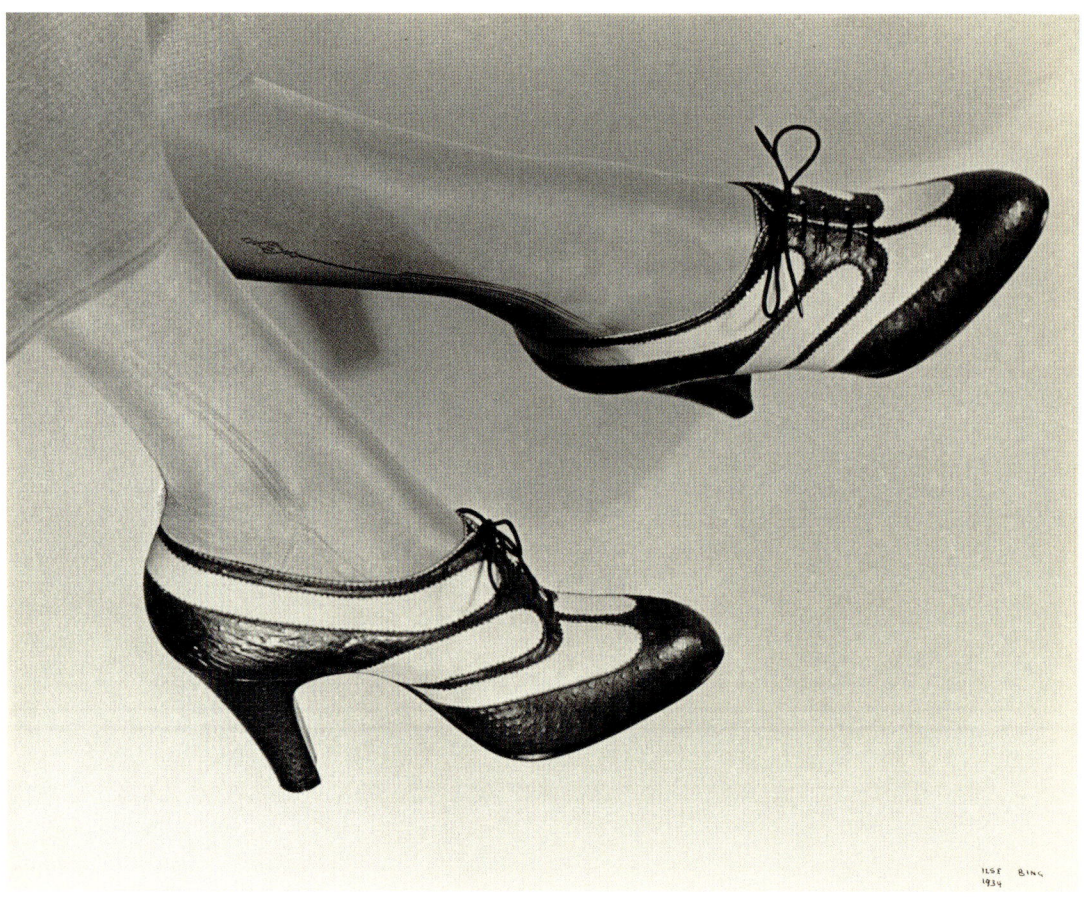

FIGURE 18
Model's Feet Wearing Two-Toned Shoes, 1934. Ilse Bing (American, 1899–1998). Gelatin silver print; image: 22.2 × 28 cm. The Cleveland Museum of Art, Gift of George Stephanopoulos, 2014.532. © Estate of Ilse Bing.

Let's consider two fashion photographs that predate *Cure/Heal* by fifty-plus years. Though one depicts a pair of heels and the other a pair of flats, fine art and commercial fashion photographer Ilse Bing's 1930s photographs *Model's Feet Wearing Two-Toned Shoes* [fig. 18] and *Gold Lamé Shoes for Harper's Bazaar* [fig. 19], which I saw for the first time in the recent Cleveland Museum of Art (CMA) exhibition *Ilse Bing: Queen of the Leica*, immediately come to mind as I gaze at Simpson's screenprint.[10] At first, Bing's image of stocking-clad feet in high-heeled, wing-tipped brogues would seem to be the most synonymous with Simpson's image, but it is Bing's photograph of a shiny pair of flats that best mirrors Simpson's monochromatic image in multiple ways. Compositionally, the gold lamé tie-ups are similarly presented in a pair on a dark backdrop. Light accentuates the pearlescent quality of the lamé, its sheen made doubly potent by the sheer matte of a pleated skirt, its folds resting in dark contrast on the model's alabaster ankles, which are covered in pale stockings. Bing's and Simpson's pictures use controlled interplay between light and shadow, matte and shine, to render materiality and fabrication in voluptuous detail. Both deemphasize function and emphasize form. For example, the lack of human presence in *Cure/Heal*, combined with its mysterious staging and dramatic lighting, draws greater attention to the curvilinear shapes of the shoes than to how or when one might wear them.

Shoes are arguably the primary subject of each image. However the figural presence in Bing's photograph marks an important compositional and conceptual distinction in relation to the figural absence in *Cure/Heal*, as does the inclusion of text in the latter. In Bing's photograph, gold lamé, most often used for special occasion wear due to its shine and fragility, glistens under studio light. The model's languid pose, coupled with the textile's preciousness, frustrates any sense of the shoes' utility, linking them in potential

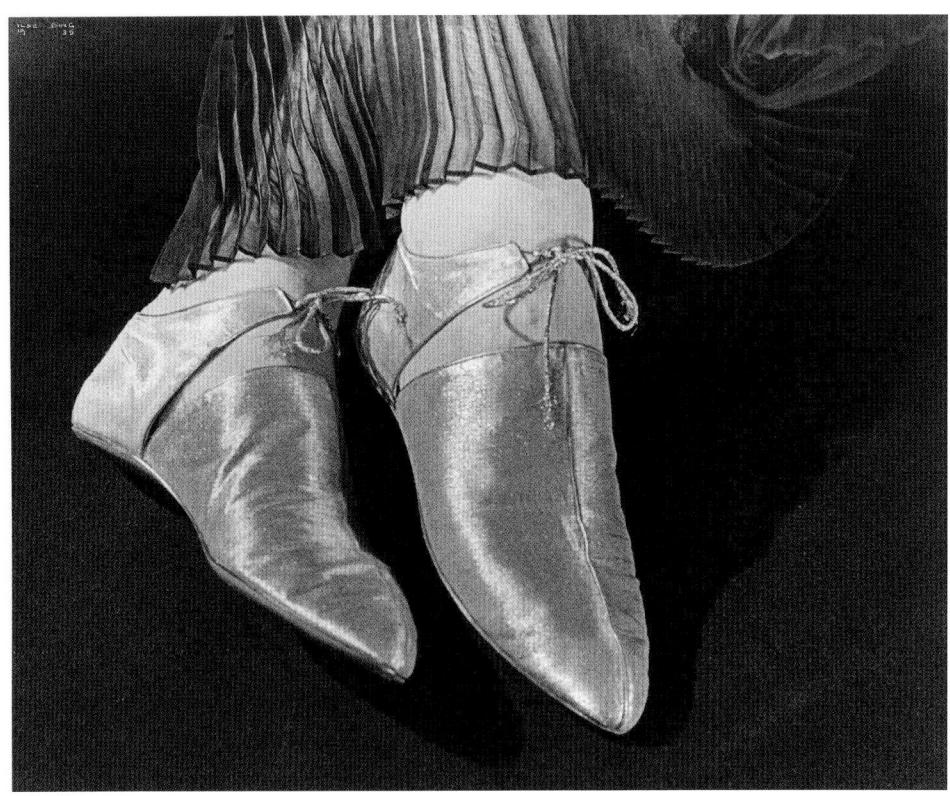

FIGURE 19
Gold Lamé Shoes for Harper's Bazaar, 1935. Ilse Bing. Gelatin silver print; image: 24 × 30.2 cm. The Cleveland Museum of Art, Gift of Michael Mattis and Judith Hochberg, 2020.292. © Estate of Ilse Bing.

non-usefulness—not to be confused with uselessness—to Simpson's shoes. Importantly, though, the model's feet, however relaxed, vivify Bing's shoes. Add to this their frontal positioning, with each foot showing a slightly different perspective and thus offering more visual detail, and their use as a foot covering, something meant to be in contact with the body, is reaffirmed. No matter that we cannot see above the figure's ankles, the presence of feet reinvigorates the shoes' capacity for movement. I imagine these feet sliding across the fabric ground and each other, the tightly woven surface and metallic threads of the lamé sliding and stuttering against raised seams. With motion, sound is activated. And I imagine ankles uncrossing and crossing again with the subtle rasp of stockings against the skirt's stiff pleats as the expensiveness and fragility of these fabrics reemphasize the preciousness of the shoes, and thus the privilege of the wearer, displayed in Bing's fashion photograph. Note that without the presence of feet—and ankles around which to secure the delicate laces—these shoes would completely lose their form. In this way, they actually need direct involvement of the human body, the addition of flesh, to invigorate them and enliven the composition.

In contrast, the pair in *Cure/Heal*, which are void of a human animating presence, stand of their own accord, allowing for far wider projections of who, in terms of class and gender, might fill them, as well as inviting us to question whether they need to be filled at all. Rather than emphasizing the utilitarian potential of footwear, as Bing's photo does, Simpson's image emphasizes human absence and objective presence. She renders these shoes especially strange by turning them away, accentuating the potential for a liberatory set of relations between viewer and picture. In this way, her suede shoes open a greater number of potential associations than do Bing's. For instance, the blend of upscale fabrics and the perceived whiteness of the model's delicate ankles, so daintily

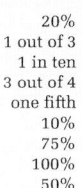
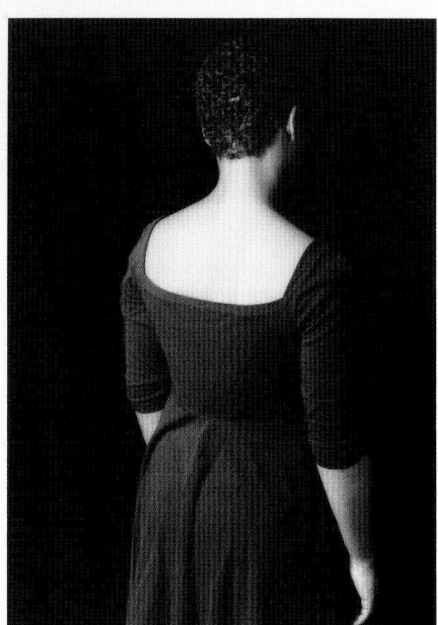
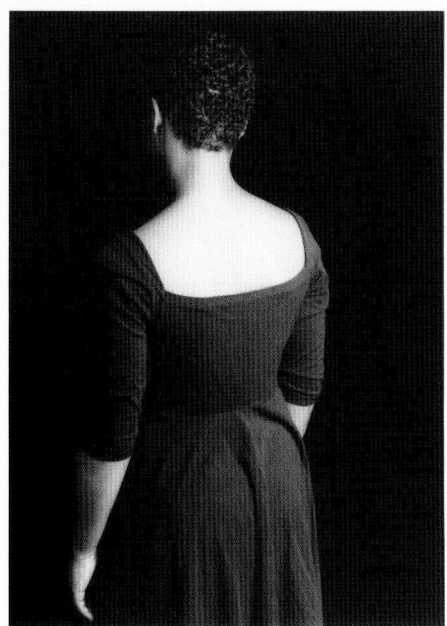

20%
1 out of 3
1 in ten
3 out of 4
one fifth
10%
75%
100%
50%

intermittent
daily
slow
for the time being
nightly
up to now
against
in the meantime
weekly
fast
throughout
spend
constant

FIGURE 20
Partitions & Time
(from the portfolio "In a Dream You Saw a Way to Survive and You Were Full of Joy, by Photographers + Friends United Against AIDS), 1991. Lorna Simpson. Gelatin silver print; image: 50.8 x 61.5 cm. The Cleveland Museum of Art, Anonymous Donor and Photographers + Friends United Against AIDS, 1995.204.4. © Lorna Simpson, courtesy of the artist and Hauser & Wirth.

crossed, seem to anchor associations with upper-class whiteness that Simpson's shoes avoid. Further, the richness of the fabrication, toe-forward positioning, and clarity of focus in Bing's photograph similarly push the viewer out of the frame just as the visual opacity and turned-away position of Simpson's invites us in, however complicatedly. As my opening recollection makes clear, it is our positionality that determines how we perceive *Cure/Heal*. But in order to advance a deeper consideration of that screenprint, I turn to a photograph subtitled *Partitions & Time* (1991) [fig. 20] that Simpson created only a year prior, which more readily epitomizes her oeuvre and from which I see *Cure/Heal* as a radical extension.

THE RÜCKENFIGUR & THE ANTIPORTRAIT

Simpson gained early acclaim for her image/text works like *Guarded Conditions* and *Partitions & Time* because of the productive ambiguities and tensions they embody. In *Partitions & Time,* which is drawn from a portfolio titled *In a Dream You Saw a Way to Survive and You Were Full of Joy* (1991), created to raise funds for the not-for-profit organization Photographers + Friends United Against AIDS, we find what has become one of Simpson's signatures: the *rückenfigur,* or figure seen from behind, paired with text that doesn't align—at least not in any simple, narrative way—with the images.[11] Here, the two central panels each feature a single figure clad in a plain black, square-backed dress, turning toward an utterly black background. While the dress and close-cropped curls may provoke multiple and perhaps conflicting assumptions about the figure's identity, those assumptions are deliberately left unresolved. Light sweeps evenly across the image, accentuating the garment's pleats and wrinkles and highlighting the figure's nape, back, and arms. The photographs are mirror images of each other; the figures, who stand at opposite angles, form a subtle *V* shape at the center of the composition.

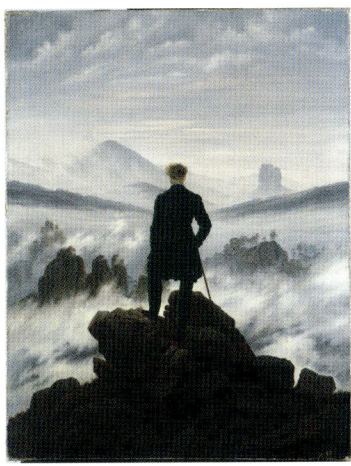

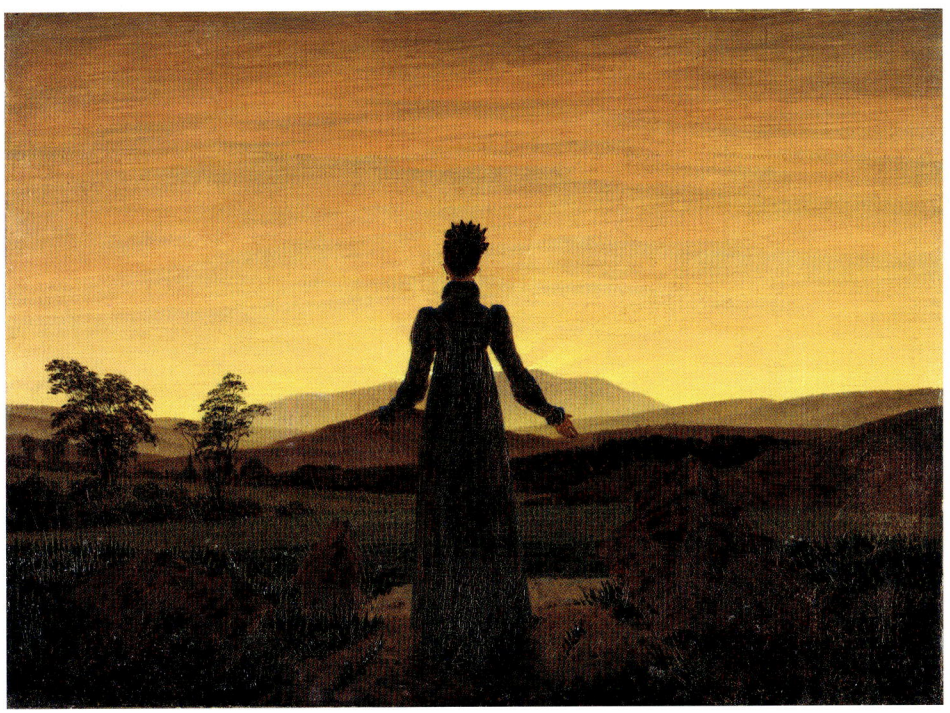

FIGURE 21
Wanderer above the Sea of Fog, c. 1817. Caspar David Friedrich (German, 1774–1840). Oil on canvas; 94.8 cm x 74.8 cm. On permanent loan from the Foundation for the Promotion of the Hamburg Art Collections. Hamburger Kunsthalle, Inv. 5161. Photo: bpk Bildagentur / Hamburger Kunsthalle / Elke Walford / Art Resource, New York.

FIGURE 22
Woman before the Rising Sun (Woman before the Setting Sun), 1818. Caspar David Friedrich. Oil on canvas; 22 x 30.5 cm. Museum Folkwang, Essen, Inv. G 45. Photo: HIP / Art Resource, New York.

The central gulley between them intimates the gutter of a book, a suggestion that is heightened by the black text that runs vertically, poetically, in the broad white margins on either side of the panels. Percentages and proportions are on the left and temporal notations are on the right. The images are immediately related to each other, but how they correspond to the texts is unclear. *Partitions & Time* leaves us to reckon with this bold disjuncture. As we shall see, the moment the artist's nebulous texts are placed in proximity to multiple and mirrored images, she summons senses beyond sight and, as coordinating and contradicting meanings proliferate, her works demand an address akin to, yet markedly different from, that of the traditional *rückenfigur*.

Although he was not the first to employ it, the *rückenfigur* was popularized in the early 1800s by German painter Caspar David Friedrich, who again and again featured figures turned away from the viewer to survey vast landscapes, as exemplified in *Wanderer above the Sea of Fog* (c. 1817) [fig. 21] and *Woman before the Rising Sun (Woman before the Setting Sun)* (1818–20) [fig. 22]. In the lush romantic landscapes and highly detailed interiors in which they reside, Friedrich's *rückenfiguren* mediate the viewer's perception, directing our attention to sublime nature and allowing us to identify with/as them because access to their actual identities is denied. This places us both inside and outside the frame and destabilizes our perceptions by dividing our focus between figure and landscape.[12] In *Wanderer*, for instance, as art historian Julian Jason Haladyn notes,

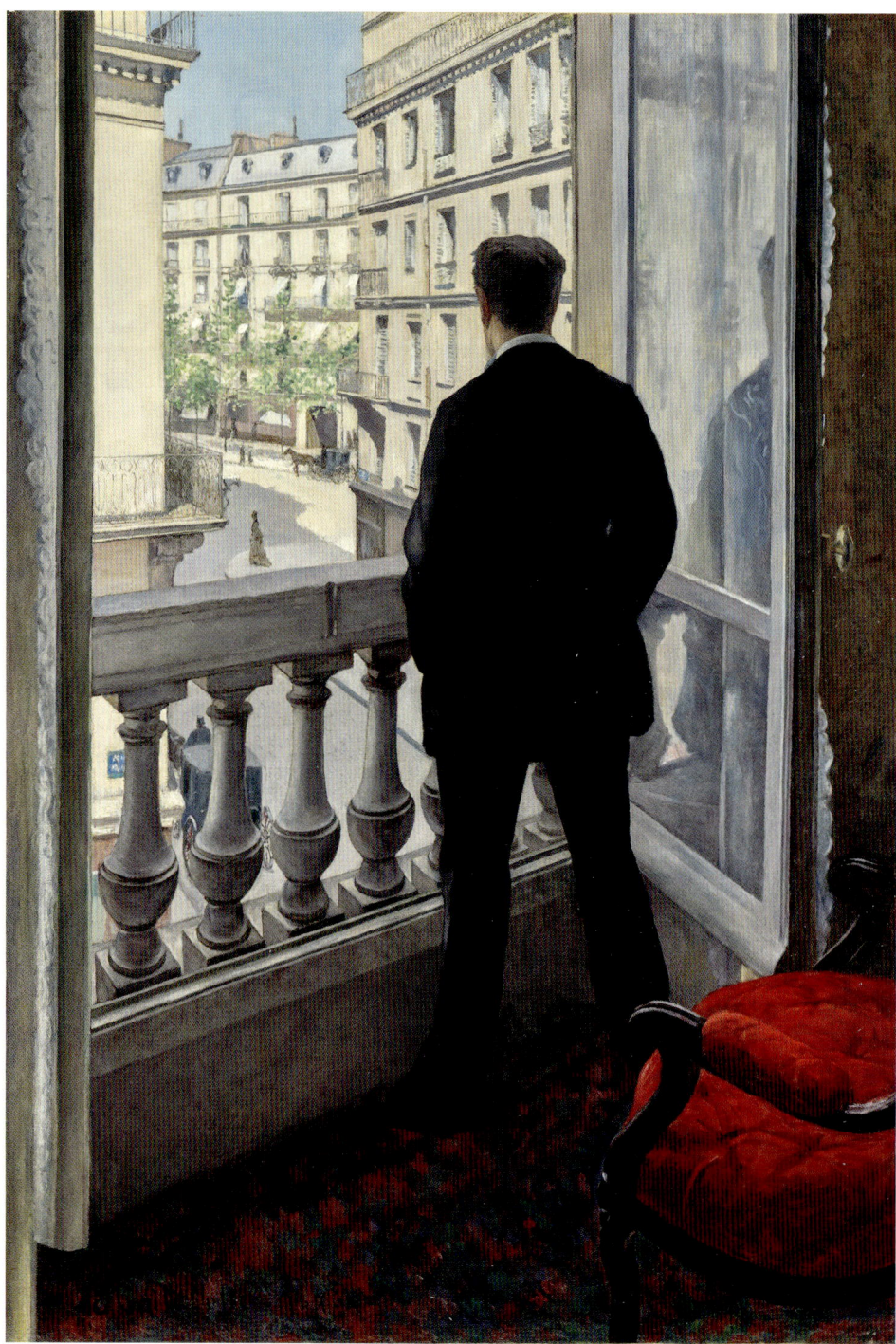

FIGURE 23
Young Man at the Window, 1876. Gustave Caillebotte (French, 1848–1894). Oil on canvas; 116 cm x 81 cm. The J. Paul Getty Museum, Los Angeles, 2021.67.

"separating the figure and the rock of the foreground from the foggy mountainous background is an indistinct and undifferentiated spatial zone that we as viewers are unable to quantify or locate within the usual imagined perspectival constructions of such a scene." Haladyn points out how these constructions work to produce the viewer's sense of the sublime by emphasizing the limits of our control, even if only perceptual, over the vast wildness of nature.[13] This motif was not exclusive to Friedrich—it can be seen throughout art history, including in the work of nineteenth-century Impressionist Gustave Caillebotte [fig. 23] and early twentieth-century Surrealist Salvador Dalí [fig. 24]. The visual impact of single figures confronting expansive views has aided in building the *rückenfigur*'s popularity over time, and although it has not been used exclusively to depict white figures, both the artists and the subjects that have drawn the most study have been overwhelmingly white and male, with previous analyses of the productive ambiguities surrounding *rückenfiguren* leaving the impact of these figures' race and gender largely unexamined.

As we shall see, though Black *rückenfiguren* are rarer than white ones, they are present in works such as the undated 1970s and 1980s self-portraits of Antiguan and German

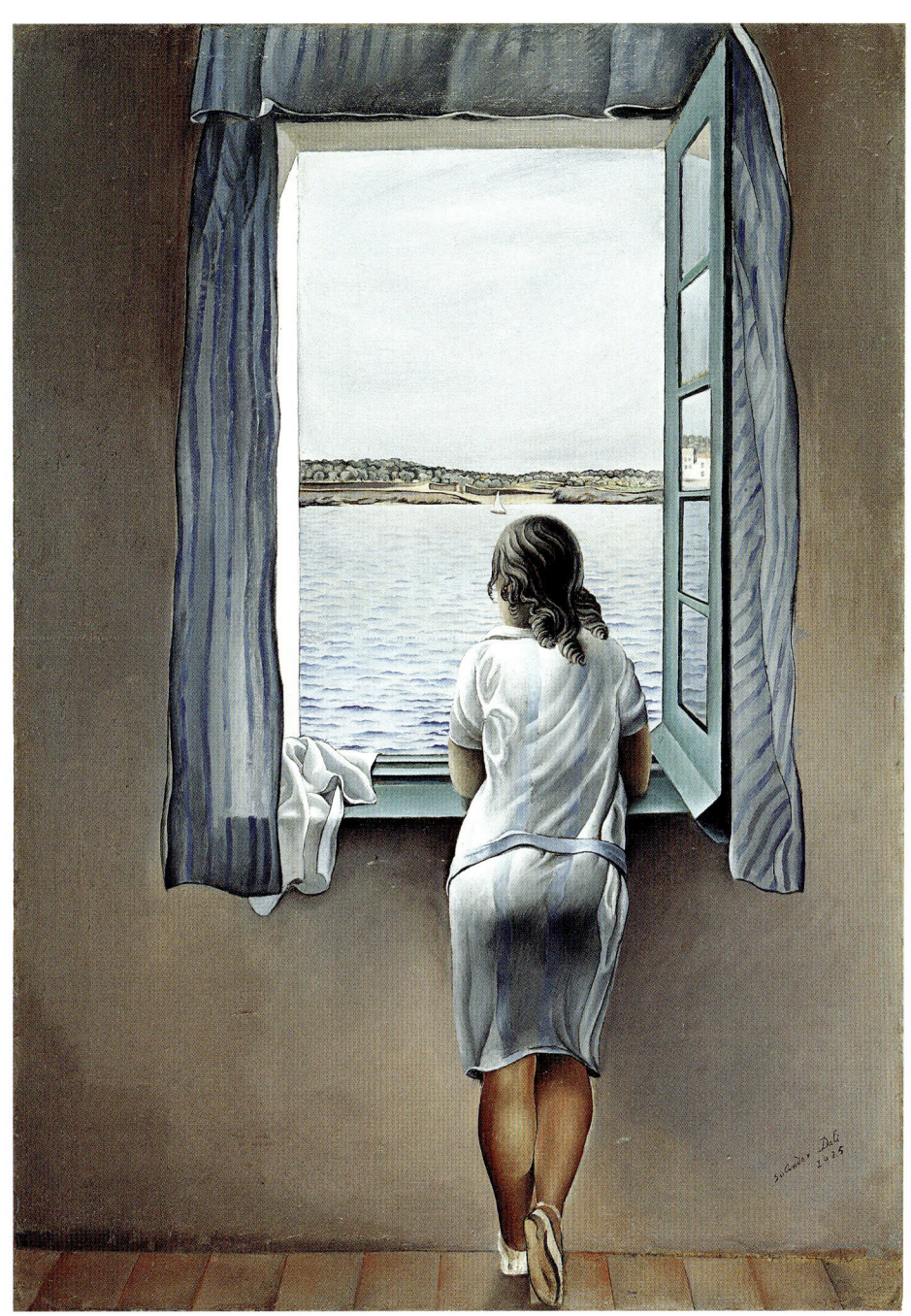

FIGURE 24
***Figura en una finestra* (Figure at the Window)**, 1925. Salvador Dalí (Spanish, 1904–1989). Oil on papier-mâché; 105 x 74.5 cm. Museo Reina Sofia, AS02157. © 2022 Salvador Dalí, Fundació Gala-Salvador Dalí, Artists Rights Society, New York

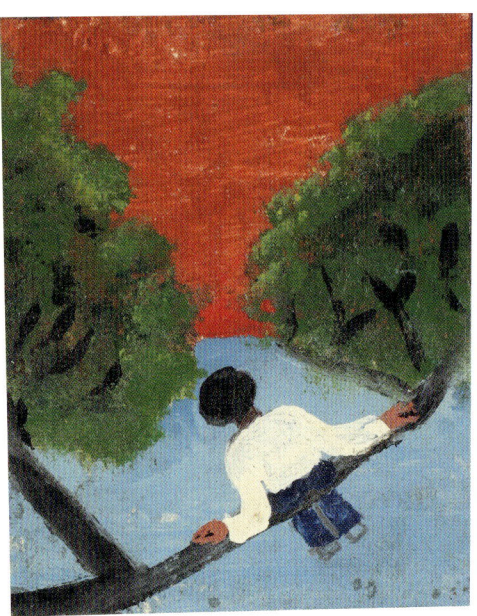

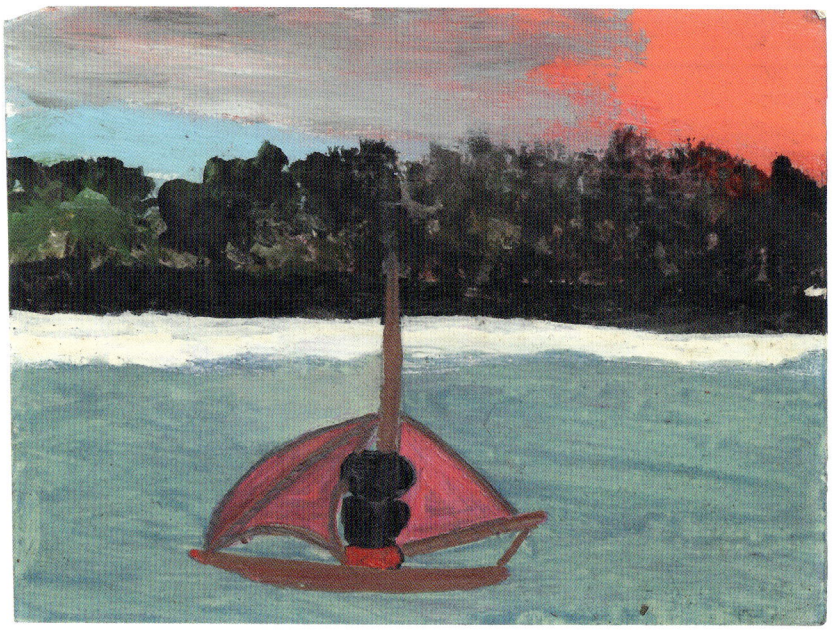

FIGURE 25
Untitled (Self-portrait in a Tree), undated. Frank Walter (Antiguan, 1926–2009). Oil on back of a Polaroid Film Box Cardstock that was formerly glued to beige Cardstock; 9.8 x 8 cm. © Kenneth M. Milton, Fine Arts Conservator

FIGURE 26
Untitled (Purple Sail Red Trunks), undated (likely 1970s or 1980s). Frank Walter. Oil on card; 13 x 18 cm. © Kenneth M. Milton, Fine Arts Conservator.

artist Frank Walter that seem to presage Simpson's contribution in really interesting ways [figs. 25 and 26]. Taking up scholarly comparisons of the "melancholic hum" of Walter's works and the tenor of Friedrich's, art historian Krista Thompson advances a consideration of Walter's self-portraits as a variant of the conventional *rückenfigur*, arguing that he offers a "grappling with how to envision, inscribe, or think more expansively about the place or non-place of Black, mixed-race, and Caribbean people in different geographic locations and landscapes," in contrast to Friedrich's more possessive views. Thompson further recognizes Walter's practice of making paintings on the backs of photographs he had taken as another way of expanding, or "refiguring" the *rückenfigur*. Thompson maintains that because these works are double-sided and as such require viewers to "flip or shift their perspectives," they "underscore broadly how a dual perspective on art and art history might be needed in order to bring overlooked histories, histories legible on, or from 'the underside,' into consideration . . . [and] prompt an expansive approach to art in that [they require] viewers to perceive multiple landscapes, mediums, and artistic forms simultaneously, or at the very least, to see them as having an intimate relationship with each other."[14]

The effects of Walter's doubling are also found in Simpson's double(d) figures, which separate her work from that of some early twentieth-century photographers, like Man

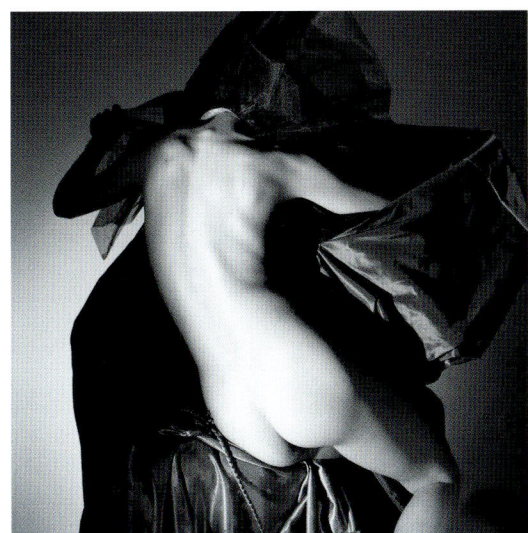
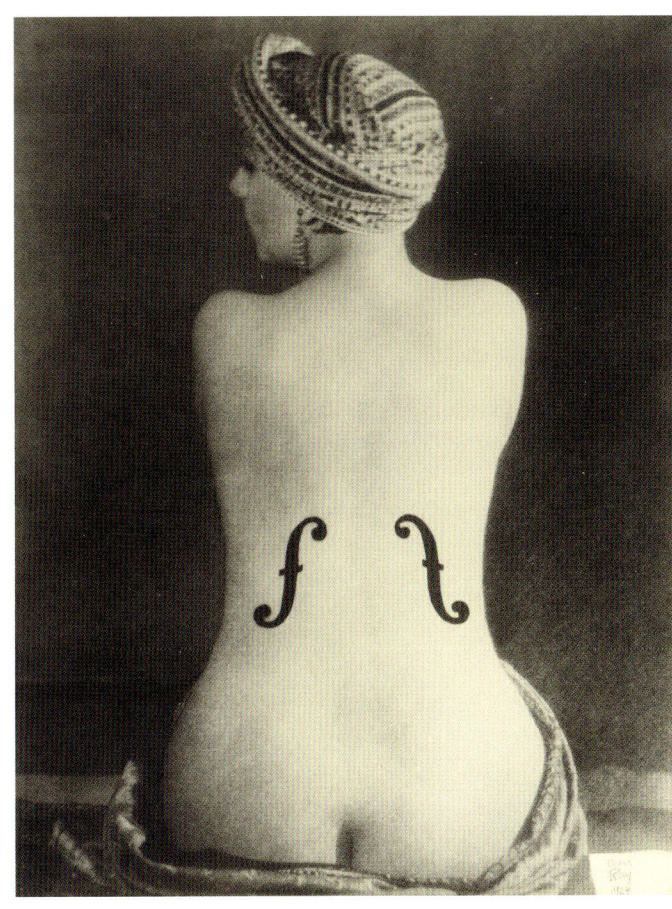

Ray's *Le Violon d'Ingres* (Ingres's Violin) [fig. 27], and from contemporary photographic considerations of the device produced in the 1980s, like Horst P. Horst's *American Nude* [fig. 28]. But both Man Ray's and Horst's images provide some semblance of a background against which to locate their figures. And, in the case of his ode to Ingres, Man Ray provides the viewer a hint at the figure's identity by showing her full profile. In each of these examples it is a male artist who controls what is and is not shown. Simpson is equally muscular in her control, but the architecture of refusal that she builds is differentiated by the culture out of which it emerges. Therefore, I see Simpson's use of the multiple in tandem with the away-facing figure as both tethered to and exceeding the lineage of the *rückenfigur*. Like Friedrich's, her figures become sometime surrogates, and she, like Walter, consistently presents Black figures in this posture. But her inclusion of Black women as *rückenfiguren* and her way of eliminating the background as a stable point of reference makes Simpson's use of the device unique in both subject-matter and presentation.

Regarding Simpson's early assemblage *Guarded Conditions*, Copeland, borrowing a term coined by curator Lauri Firstenberg, speaks to the generative uncertainties found in Simpson's work when he calls the eighteen Polaroids "antiportraits," noting their "refusal of the gaze" and "denial of presumed access to a subject."[15] Simpson's works likewise present a proliferation of refusals, multiplying the away-facing Black feminine figure, juxtaposing it with text, setting it before a void, and thus making antiportraits of what I have described as her *rückenfiguren*. For instance, the lack of correspondence between the figures and texts in *Partitions & Time* places its subjects outside of the typical exchange between object and viewer. In some ways this lack of clarity is like the dense fog in Friedrich's *Wanderer* in that it produces both spatial and temporal uncertainties that play with our perceptions. However, these figures aren't an intermediary to sublime nature

FIGURE 27
Le Violon d'Ingres
(Ingres's Violin), 1924.
Man Ray (American, 1860–1976). Gelatin silver print re-worked with pencil and ink; 29.6 x 22.7 cm. J. Paul Getty Museum, 86.XM.626.10. © Man Ray 2015 Trust / Artists Rights Society (ARS), New York / ADAGP, Paris 2022

FIGURE 28
American Nude, 1982.
Horst P. Horst (German American, 1906–1999). Platinum-palladium print; 63.5 x 61 cm. Private collection. © Condé Nast

and we are not invited to imagine what they see, and thus they are less suitable as the kind of universal surrogate that *rückenfiguren* like Friedrich's aspired to be. Therefore, I'd like to suggest that Simpson's figures are nonutilitarian in ways that make them more similar to the shoes presented in *Cure/Heal*, which are further clarified by the mutual visual resistances they pose, and that their refusal to serve as surrogates for any but a very specific set of viewers connects them to a particularly Black and particularly female culture of dissemblance.

LIBERATORY DISSEMBLANCE: WHAT LIES BETWEEN CARING AND MENDING?

As the evacuated background frees the figures in *Partitions & Time* from the confines of a particular geography or temporal framing and simultaneously offers them a protective layer of anonymity and mystery, so too does the double void—of the missing human figure and the impenetrably dark background—presented in *Cure/Heal* traffic in what has been termed a culture of dissemblance. This descriptor was originally used by historian Darlene Clark Hine to characterize "the behavior and attitudes of Black women that created the appearance of openness and disclosure but actually shielded the truth of their inner lives and selves from their oppressors."[16] Hine saw dissemblance as a direct by-product of the "ever-present threat and reality of rape," domestic violence, and economic oppression to which Black women have been subjected from the antebellum period to the present.[17] This condition simultaneously produced "efforts to resist the misappropriation and to maintain the integrity of their own sexuality" and ultimately informed social protest and motivated Black migrations.[18] In the three decades since Hines exposed this thread in Black women's narratives, the concept of Black dissemblance as both shield and sword of Black liberation has been broadly utilized and expanded, as well as critiqued. What has remained constant, however, is the potential for freedom to be found through both insistent interiority and concealment. In other words, refusing unrestricted access to one's body, to one's thoughts, to one's joy and pain, are ways to gain power.

Compositional symmetries abound between *Partitions & Time* and *Cure/Heal,* including the oblique angles at which the figures in the first composition, and the shoes in the second, are placed; the tenebrous emptiness into which both recede; and the complex juxtapositions of image and text that define each. Together, these three features create an insistent interiority, a multifaceted set of refusals characteristic of antiportraits. The essence of this insistent interiority may be properly located in what curator and critic Joan Simon describes as the "resonant gap" that is ever-present in Simpson's oeuvre. Simon defines this space as one that "invites the viewer/reader to enter, all the while requiring an active reckoning with some inalienable truths: seeing is not necessarily believing and what we might see is altered not only by our individual experiences and assumptions, but also critically by what we might hear."[19] Simon helpfully introduces ideas of concealment via photographic and textual artifice as well as a text's potential to represent sound, thereby re-exposing the duplicitous nature of the photographic image as well as the possible multisensory impact of a two-dimensional work. She also introduces the slash as a *break* between words, signifying more than one kind of relationship between them. This is especially important to an analysis of dissemblance in *Cure/Heal,* whose two hovering blood-red words are punctuated by a slash that destabilizes their relationship with each other and with the image they ostensibly describe.

The verb "dissemble" means to hide under a false appearance, put on the appearance of something, or conceal facts, intentions, or feelings under some pretense. Thus, the seemingly straightforward titular relationship of text to image in the screenprint mirrors precisely the terms of concealment and disclosure in Hine's description of dissemblance: the words that at first appear to name the image instead conceal a plethora of relations that can be known only through scholarly investigation and personal reflection, acts that will never reveal all possible meanings. This doesn't mean we shouldn't seek these meanings; rather. it means we should never be satisfied that what we've sought, nor what we gain, is complete. There's no such thing and the reward is in the effort. Both "Cure" and "Heal" feel declarative, even without a "to" preceding either and making it infinitive and thus binding it to a particular subject. Together they demand that we cure and/or heal. But cure/heal what, or whom? The connection between these terms may appear matter-of-fact, in that to cure something often means to heal it, and vice versa, but an etymological analysis of the two words offers a more complex account of their meaning individually and as a pair. "Cure" comes from the Latin *cura,* or "care," and *curare*, "to care for." "Heal" comes from the Old English *hælan*, meaning "to restore to sound health." Care hasn't the resolved quality of cure, as the latter suggests the elimination of an ailment, while the former suggests an attending to or nurturing of an ailment *in the hopes* of eliminating it. One is a state and the other a striving; one suggests finality, the other suggests flux. And if to heal is to restore health there is an inherent sense of repair, or mending, that may gesture toward wholeness, but with an ever-present possibility of damage. Both words contain within them a sense of tending to what is broken, and much more meaning can be found in the break between them.

Notice how the slash rests just at the center of the composition. Coupled with the positioning of the shoes away from each other, its placement suggests that something exists between the caring and the mending implied by the text. The teetering posture that high heels require does in fact cause physical harm to the wearer over time; perhaps it is this that needs a cure or to be healed. Or perhaps the denial of a body upon which to hang assumptions of gender, class, or race is a call to attend to how easily we might otherwise make those assumptions. Then, upon even closer inspection, notice the space that hovers between the *E* in "cure" and the *H* in "heal." These spaces are broader than those between the individual letters. Here the resonant gap feels like a caesura, defined as a pause or a break in a line or verse of poetry. A caesura can be thought of as a predetermined visual, temporal, and physical pause in a text. These multifaceted gaps open onto different realms of knowledge just as they impose constrictions on any sense of complete knowledge. Instead, they ask us to witness the gap as a part of knowledge. In other words, the caesurae between "cure" and "heal" suggest a network of contingencies that shift depending upon the viewer/reader. In this way, what is found through any mining of the resonant gap, as one might investigate literary caesura, will relate directly to the positionality of the analyst. As such, every projection that I've made in this essay is simultaneously contingent upon immediate and past experiences, that which I remember and that which I have forgotten, that which I can research and that which cannot be found in the archive. I believe that Simpson's method for generating an economy of secrecy includes the strategic appearance of openness. By this I don't mean that her works appear easy, but rather that there are important pathways of interpretation that reside at the surface and only reveal their limitations once mined. In other words, they make you work to get to . . . more work. This is not to say that the nineteenth- and twentieth-century *rückenfiguren* to which I've referred are somehow doing less. I simply think they are doing differently and asking different questions. So, in addition to speaking to me of Black American womanhood and our continued necessity for dissemblance, they also speak to the necessity of multidimensional (read: wide-ranging, interdisciplinary, and nonlinear) forms of address advanced by as many minds as possible.

Right now, the demand for personal transparency in professional spaces is at an all-time high. I wonder at the ways in which Black people, and Black women in particular, are being asked to reveal our pain in unmediated ways in order to build "empathy," without any consideration of how hard-won our privacy might be and how effective a space apart might be in processing our collective trauma, yes, but also our collective joy, without scrutiny. When the visual markers of freedom that have been provided do not meet the needs of the people they are meant to represent, new ones must be conceived. Simpson's ability to make these stakes visible for Black women is unique. However, the *rückenfigur* cum antiportrait *Cure/Heal* is but one example that captures the ineffable nature of Black (non)belonging, by which I mean the interstitial status between belonging and not belonging that seems to be our perpetual state in the United States and beyond.

I conclude with a neon work by artist Glenn Ligon, *Rückenfigur*, from 2009 [fig. 29], which refers to a famous Charles Dickens line: "It was the best of times, it was the worst of times." Ligon says, "I realized, actually, Dickens is talking about a moment that society is in where everything is happening and nothing is happening; everything is booming and everyone is poor. . . . The dichotomies . . . seemed, to me, embodied in the word 'America.'"[20] Here the word is the *rückenfigur* turning away from us, but as the artist notes it simultaneously faces us, making itself strange. Ligon's neon composition forces a pause as things go "wrong" at the middle of the word, where the space between two electrical cords marks the space between the backward *E* and *R* and heightens the sense of duality that the artist not only wants to make us aware of but also asks us to dwell in.

The lack of a human figure (besides an implied viewer), as well as the resonant gap produced by refiguring the letters and changing the expected presentation of a word, connect Ligon's *Rückenfigur* to Simpson's *Cure/Heal*, in that viewers are unable to anchor, in any finalizing way, all of the nuanced relations to be found in and through either work. It is also the case that both point to the complex status of Black people within structures that are glacially slow to change, if not intransigent. And they importantly make visible the gap between what is shown and what is known. Instead of providing clear answers, each evokes more questions, and each resists any desire for an easy summation of meaning.

It is necessary for museums as educational and civic spaces to provide frameworks and insights that offer information and inspiration and do not foreclose wonder. I hope that in these pages I have provided a roadmap to visual analysis that takes seriously both the archival and the visceral connections possible when we allow a single work to inspire our investigations. In this essay I've created a network of interpretation that includes links to works within an artist's body of work, among multiple objects in the CMA's and other collections, and within scholarly literature and poetry. I've also spent considerable time on an ekphrastic interpretation as well as on personal connections to the objects and theories I've included. All of this points to both the rigor and the inherent limitations of this work. This is not meant to be a universal or final interpretation. Rather than coming to a single conclusion that aims to prevent critique or preclude other interpretations, this work is meant to provide one route to a comportment of openness necessary to meeting some of art's demands for inquiry.

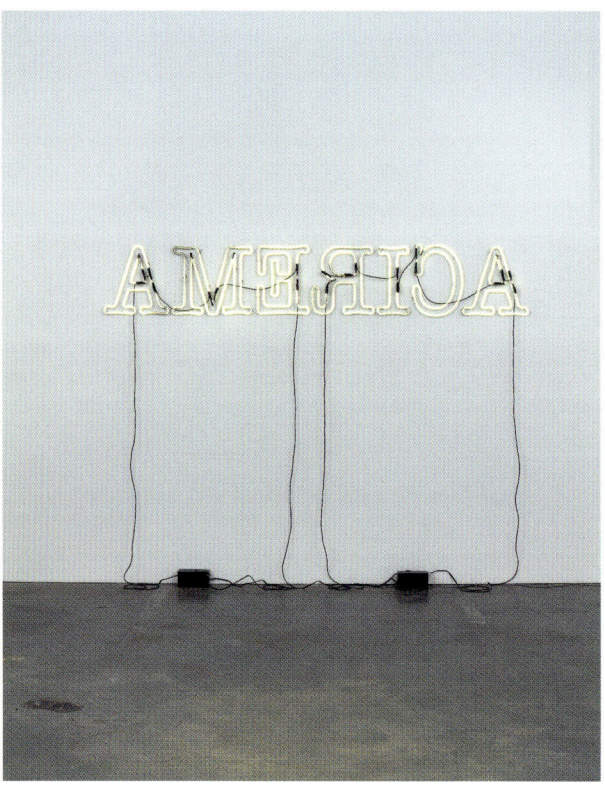

FIGURE 29
Glenn Ligon
Rückenfigur, 2009.
Neon and paint;
61 x 368.3 x 10.2 cm.
Edition of 3 and 2 APs
© Glenn Ligon; Courtesy of the artist, Hauser & Wirth, New York, Regen Projects, Los Angeles, Thomas Dane Gallery, London and Galerie Chantal Crousel, Paris.

1. Margo Jefferson, "Lorna Simpson: Pictures," *Aperture* 223 (Summer 2016): 73–75.

2. Huey Copeland, "Lorna Simpson's Figurative Transitions," in *Bound to Appear: Art, Slavery, and the Site of Blackness in Multicultural America* (Chicago: University of Chicago Press, 2013), 65.

3. Simpson's is one of ten works in the portfolio *10: The Artist as Catalyst*, published in 1992 to support the Alternative Museum, described on the Cleveland Museum of Art website as "an experimental New York exhibition venue . . . [that] aimed to address inequity in the art world. . . ." See "10: The Artist as Catalyst, *Cure/Heal* by Lorna Simpson, Cleveland Museum of Art, accessed December 18, 2021, https://www.clevelandart.org/art/2019.73.4. The portfolio also includes photographs and prints by Luis Cruz Azaceta, Ida Applebroog, Leon Albert Golub, Luis Alfonso Jiménez, Jerry Byron Kearns, Vitaly Komar, Adrian Piper, Ben Sakoguchi, and Andres Serrano.

4. Some families, especially those educated and/or freed under slavery, kept lists of births, deaths, and marriages passed down to each new generation. I have yet to locate such a text, or any mention of it, for either side of my family.

5. Some place the invention of high heels as early as c. 300 BC because there is evidence that ancient Egyptian butchers used high heels to keep their feet dry as they worked. See Harish V. Kurup, Callum I. M. Clark, and Raman K. Dega, "Footwear and orthopaedics," *Foot and Ankle Surgery* 18, no. 2 (June 2012): 79–83. Available online at https://www.sciencedirect.com/science/article/pii/S1268773111000476.

6. See "Standing TALL: The Curious History of Men in Heels," curated by the Bata Shoe Museum, Toronto, for a Google Arts & Culture visual timeline, accessed November 27, 2021, https://artsandculture.google.com/exhibit/BQJSZR_j5AhtLA.

7. Ibid.

8. Ibid.

9. Ibid.

10. *Ilse Bing: Queen of the Leica*, Cleveland Museum of Art, March 7–October 11, 2020, curated by Barbara Tannenbaum.

11. Although its title extends to a portfolio of works by twelve artists, "In a Dream You Saw a Way to Survive and You Were Full of Joy" is credited to artist Jenny Holzer, who debuted the phrase in her *Survival Series* (1983–85), which was shown on large electronic billboards in public spaces. In the portfolio it appears twice: on the foil-stamped cloth that covers the portfolio box and as a cast aluminum plaque within it. The portfolio also includes editioned photographs by David and Peter McGough, Tina Barney, Lorna Simpson, Sarah Charlesworth, Thomas Ruff, Andres Serrano, Jeff Wall, Alfredo Jaar, James Welling, Frank Majore, and Joel-Peter Witkin.

12. For more on how the *rückenfigur* toggles attention between figure and scene, see Geoffrey D. Schott, "The *Rückenfigur*: A Note on an Intriguing Rear-View Pictorial Device," *Perception* 49, no. 5 (May 2020): 600–605.

13. Julian Jason Haladyn, "Friedrich's 'Wanderer': Paradox of the Modern Subject," *RACAR: Revue d'art Canadienne / Canadian Art Review* 41, no. 1 (2016): 47–61.

14. Krista Thompson, "History on the Underside: Refiguring the Rückenfigur in Frank Walter's Landscapes and Photographs," in *Frank Walter: A Retrospective*, ed. Barbara Paca and Susanne Pfeffer (Frankfurt am Main: Museum für moderne Kunst, 2020), 371–72.

15. See Copeland, *Bound to Appear*, 65.

16. Darlene Clark Hine, "Rape and the Inner Lives of Black Women in the Middle West," *Signs* 14, no. 4 (1989): 912–20.

17. Ibid.

18. Ibid.

19. Joan Simon, "Easy to Remember, Hard to Forget: Lorna Simpson's Gestures and Reenactments," in *Lorna Simpson*, ed. Simon (Munich: Prestel, 2013), 9.

20. Glenn Ligon, "Glenn Ligon Reframes History in the Art of 'America,'" interview by Audie Cornish for Weekend Edition, National Public Radio, May 8, 2011, transcript available at https://www.npr.org/2011/05/08/136022514/glenn-ligon-reframes-history-in-the-art-of-america.

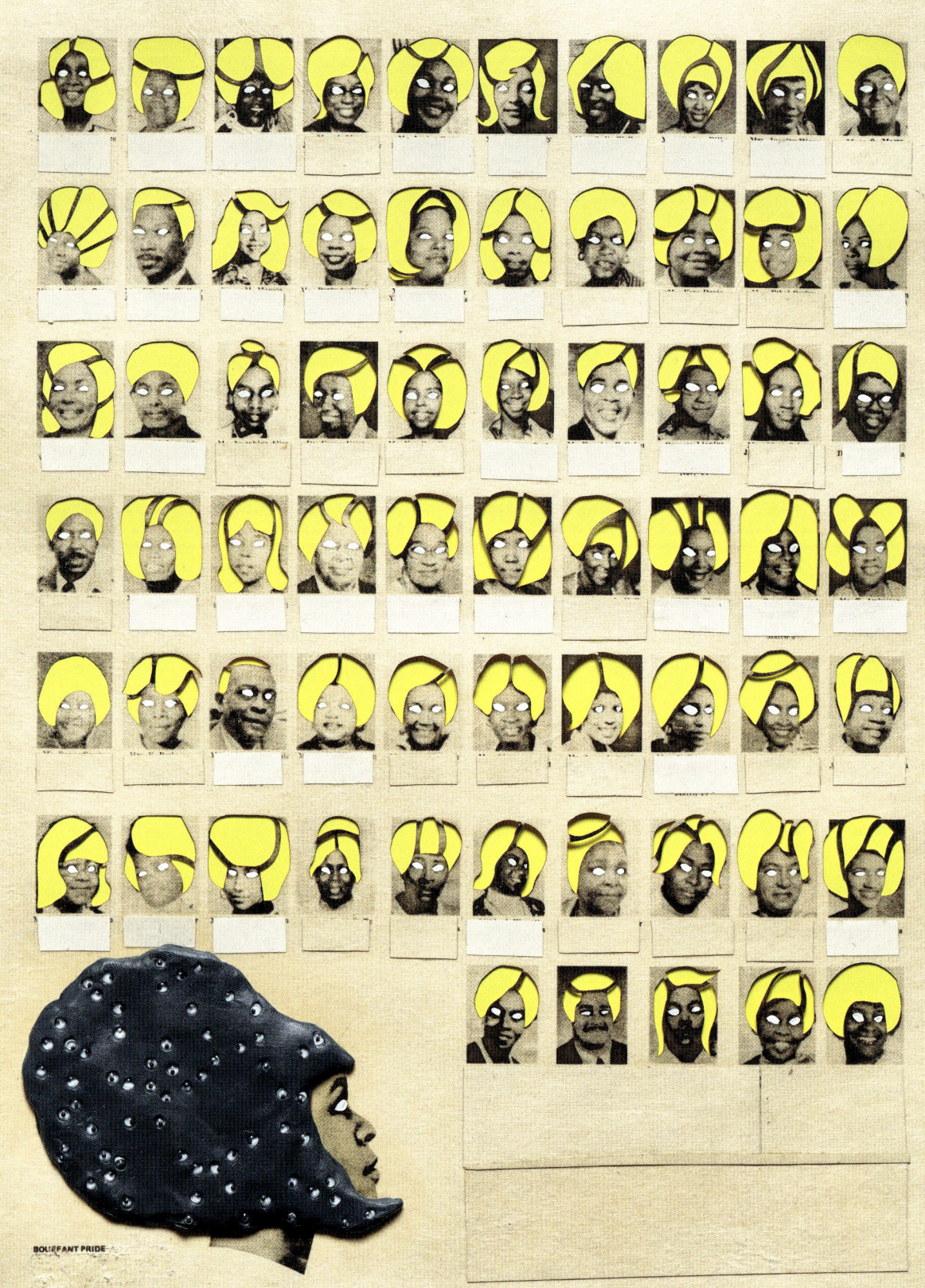

"SPIT-BITE"
ROBIN COSTE LEWIS

**NOTES IN CONVERSATION WITH
ELLEN GALLAGHER'S *BOUFFANT PRIDE*:
AN INTRODUCTION**

I don't like to speak publicly about hair. It feels too private, too intimate. For me, the old well-worn sentiment *Don't touch my hair* is just a first step—the lowest bar—kindergarten. Don't touch it—certainly. Don't touch any part of me. Don't even look at it. It isn't for you. Or you. You either. Don't look at me.

I don't know how I came to feel this way. Or better: *when*? I think it has something to do with leaving home (Los Angeles) (alone) (as a teenager) and heading to New York City to be an artist, a writer—even though, at the time, I had no idea what either of those words (*artist* or *writer*) actually meant. There was language, and there were images, constantly spiraling along my DNA, whispering and projecting.

As a child, I'd never met any formal artists; never heard of any contemporary writers. LAUSD schools, then, were exactly what they still are now: a holding place America sends its children while it continues to reckon with how to spell the word *citizen*. Just before completing high school—which is to say: before high school completed me—I left.

I didn't know it at the time, indeed it took decades for me to realize that I was—which is to say, my profound invisible life—nothing more than a distinct expression of history. There was no real *Robin*. No real *Lewis*. For the first fifty years, I believed, like everyone else, what I was taught in school: I was *an individual*. It wasn't until I grew much older, having stared that ever-shifting face in the mirror, decade after decade, that I began to realize, yet again, that I had been lied to. Who was that staring back at me? And then, sometimes, I wondered, not *Who is that*? but *What is that*?

What am I?

My mother's freckles. My grandmother's asymmetrical smile. Her bold knuckles. That thick blue vein roping across the top of her left hand also, now, ropes across mine. The gravel and Gulf shells rumbling gently beneath my voice. The way we pronounce *ambulance* and *theatre*. The just-off-center mole on all of our chests. The slow way the evolution of human language became clear to me whenever we spoke—all our history skipping and jumping rope—blackly—with white syntax.

It isn't possible to explain.

Pictures can articulate this better.

All I can say is that, even as a child, I knew our words were on the longest end of the tip of a branch of a tree that had been growing for millions of years. I could hear the firelight against a cave, see the feathers, feel the excellent, brave maritime migrations across every ocean—the evolution of tools, say—how history felt like an almost eternal straight line, every human evolution, for millions of years, and the tip of that line ended inside my mouth.

FIGURE 30
Bouffant Pride, 2003. Ellen Gallagher (American, b. 1965). Collage of photogravures, plasticine, paint, ink, and found objects; support: rag paper; sheet: 34.3 x 26.6 cm. The Cleveland Museum of Art, Judith and James Saks in memory of Lynn and Dr. Joseph Tomarkin Endowment, 2003.340. © Ellen Gallagher. Courtesy Gagosian.

That very fine sound of wet cement being spread out onto dry pavement. Its ancient technology. The sound of my Uncle Milton sharpening his knife. The vowels and consonants in his last name always made me smile: Doucette. Like the announcement of a duel. He also said son of a bitch better than any human being has ever said it—ever. The way all the women twisted their torsos away from the camera, then turned back and leaned their chins, their shoulders—but mostly their eyes—inward, toward the lens.

:

At some point, during my childhood, while everyone outside was busy pretending we weren't at war, weren't mid-escape, weren't on a battlefield, weren't trapped, weren't running away, weren't living in a place where you could wake up with all four of the walls on fire, ablaze—all the women in the neighborhood began to pull their hair.

Upward.

I remember the moment distinctly. One woman, then another, began to appear—in the vacated spaces where their old bodies had once been. My mother. My aunts. My grandmother. My grand great-aunts. The usual things they held and did began to fall away. And it was then that something inside my girl body turned around and began to look at them. Differently. I was witnessing a marriage of politics, philosophy, aesthetics. And I knew it. I just didn't know that one day I would fall upon the words that could explain it.

:

Staring at night, every night, again, I begin to wonder about them—this ancient flock of migratory birds that carried me inside their bodies for thousands of miles, until we landed here. Another ocean. Another sea. More salt. And here, staring at their lives through the darkness, I wonder—now—was this the very first time that I watched them all change, that very first moment when I realized, and they (all new Great Migration mothers) realized, too, that a woman could absolutely stop being who she was one day, then decide to become someone wholly different tomorrow. New

(All birds drop their feathers at some point. Most drop them all their lives).

Great Blue

:

Was the round tower of curls, the ongoing concentric circles built steadily but softly into one towering circle, an announcement, a tool of distraction—a way to point the world away—from what was both present and absent in their eyes? Was the new "style" similar to what Barthes said about photographs—it isn't the image that we see? Which is to say that, during the 1970s, when American Negro women stopped mimicking the older styles and began to build their hair into this proud round spire, it wasn't "just a hairstyle" that we were witnessing. It was the gendered face of history. Action. Resistance. Great Migration artifacts. New gestures of female evolution.

I knew it was a mystery, a strength, the way the World whispered to them, invited them, to inhabit even more courage—I could see the red-hot boldness in their quiet eyes—but America merely called it the bouffant.

:

Maybe.

:

Or maybe being a woman within the context of patriarchy is such a monumental mindfuck, you can be looking at yourself right in the mirror and still not have the insight to recognize the history being made by your own face. How is it possible to be certain who you are, if and when every morning when you make any kind of statement, the entire world pretends as if you haven't just spoken—and spoken clearly?

:

I used to think style, and women's style particularly, especially my own, was just individual expression. And then, at some point, I began to realize that I was a misogynist, just like everyone else, constantly minimizing or dismissing women (myself) as trite, instead of appreciating their ability to continually reach for pleasure while circling within a hot whirlpool of white shit.

Which is to say, we hear a great deal about the people on the Titanic, how brave a few were for picking up their instruments and beginning to play the cello, say, while the ship sank. Why then—on the cliffs of climate collapse, a collapse caused by colonialist gestures of empire and occupation, don't we ever express anything similar about the tenacity of Black women?

:

Another election come and gone—another country saved (again) by the quiet electoral technicians who, for generations, have braided political strategies throughout their hair, while everyone looks away, and follows in a line behind another loud white man, a good one this time, but still another loud white man, pointing and shouting.

:

It's so easy to dismiss a woman's life.

:

Even now, in 2021, when so-called "Mother's Day" rolls around (One day, really? One day?), and we bring a bouquet of flowers, or a toaster, or parade the woman who ignited the flame of our very finite breath, out to lunch—the ever grateful female prop—as if any one day per year could add up to the sacrifice called "a woman's life.

:

The way we turn. The way they pronounced the letter B—so intimate with the letter V—or the R and its long-lost evolutionary friend, the L. Or/even the way they braided our hair, palms up or down, all the international global histories that decision contains (All the vessel histories it contains, too). Sugar never in this, salt only in that—the geometry of the parting. A collective, invisible education, a critique on the individual, as prominent as any discussion ever had inside the Capitol.

:

All the "stories" we heard, and remember, when we were too young to understand what we were really listening to was the recitation of a survival manual, a manual that contained sections we could not begin to understand, until we were twenty, thirty, forty, fifty—a revelation for every decade. And then the true plot-twisting clencher, when, on the brink of sixty, you begin to realize all that came before was only their unwritten Introduction: a key to a door we have yet to realize exists. Transmission.

:

How often I wonder.

:

For every novel published, the hundreds of thousands that were never printed—
For every poem in print, the hundreds of millions more that were lost—
A whole life spent walking delightedly the halls of one long great poem—never spoken—

:

With every letter, I am attempting to hold on to those specific, exacting sensations of what it meant to be a small spark of the first generation of children in my family who were born outside of the place where we'd been born for generations. Somehow.

I am trying to remember the stories my uncle told me about how an entire neighborhood in New Orleans was built—by friends—over the weekends, acre by acre, beam by beam, each family helping the other families to save. Timber. Nails. Land.

Or: my mother's description of the rafters above her head—the hands that built them—my great-grandfather Leonce, whom I never met. All he had to do was look at a house. A few months later it's be built. Baking soda for your teeth at night instead of toothpaste—because, even then, they knew it was all a lie (Daddy then says at the table, "See, baby, their toothpaste was full of sugar!").

Or: the way the fields look in the background of the sepia-colored people smiling at me from inside a photograph—right here, right now—on my desk in front of me.

(What did they grow, in which season? And why?)

The way my father recited certain rhymes.

And—a janitor—how he loved nothing more than to talk about *pi*.

Him—then. And her. Watching them, smile, at night, in their bed. A janitor and a housewife—her hair wrapped tightly—the *bouffant*—discussing over my pretending-to-be-asleep-four-year-old-body this mathematical mystery. That is an archive.

:

I don't care any more what anyone believes about my body.

(What anyone thinks about my body isn't worthy of my attention.)

Your voice is a distraction.

Stop talking.

I only want to listen to what we think about ourselves

when you are nowhere around.

It's mine.

It's my body.

I want the syntax eyeless.

I want to preserve my sight, older than sand.

There is nothing more lovely than her voice calling me

from the other room.

ENDURE

women are quiet
regarding the silence
between us
the babies we did not
have had hated
wanted did not want
hated wanting had left
lost found fell out
down we do
not mention it
but let it float there between
us what we know don't
know pretend
not to know not to notice our
price what we will will
not sale the house the hungers
the lovers we did did
not should should not
have not had had
the book in which we hid
the book the letter
the receipt the just-
in-case money the rent
the will the real
story sometimes we
tell do not tell or
glance where we
don't will will
not might for the right
person might not tell it
floats there
there in the quiet
we don't tell tell what
we really bear like
crows we kah-kah about

nothing
when what's most
telling most raucous
within us is in us
in us most quiet
endures

(I KEEP MY OWN EMPIRES IN THE BACKGROUND AND MANAGE THEM IN SILENCE)

We plucked out our eyes and left them
    there, under the rocks—tucked—
        because we no longer wanted to see
            the approaching centuries of our long, enduring future.

Or. We plucked
    them out—because eyes were wholly unnecessary by then—
        and we could already see the entire transparent World
            (completely) without them.

And. Or.
    They also plucked at our sight, but left
        our eyes intact, so that we would only forever
            always feel the past, like an anchor, tugging beneath us,

not a prison, a burnished gift, but not a clear sail day either.
    A stationing. A waiting.
        We waited so long—staring inside, underneath—we turned
            into an entirely different creature.

Or. Perhaps it was never tragic.
    Perhaps we chose to jump into the blood,
        to see and inhabit always
            the footprint of every living cell.

HIBERNATION

I don't know how to fit back inside
the small cave. The earth

has fallen to sleep. I missed the dry signals.
Too much light has made me

sick. I am trying
to find the dark place.

[UNTITLED]

Every day
an exodus.

No origins,
no beginnings.

Vast, Black,
infinite: the Past

is endless
and still

just
departing.

THE PROCESS

An erasure of James Baldwin's
"The Creative Process"

Being alone—compelled

    to linger—to be created,

        to be physical,

to lose purpose

    (which is, after

        all), to dwell.

Birth—or Death—

    the fearless

        eyes of mystery,

of any desire. God,

    in an attempt to make vivid

        His endeavor—

extreme, universal—

    inescapable correct delusions

        we fall into. Reason

that incorrigible

    Disturber—of-the-Peace,

        that *Future-Better-Purpose-*

society chaos—in order

    to make life bearable—

        General Beginning-of-Time:

unwilling, indeed unable,

    to live without minimizing

        human damage.

However: the mystery

    of being human is stable.

        The answer hides—

a breed of honor—

    all-tender

        reality.

Peculiar nature

    never ceases warring:

        for change, for health.

Now: Love.   See

    the face,

        this face,

the most extraordinary—essentially

    rare barrier—frightened

        of precarious security.

Delicate,

    strenuous.

        Unshakable.

We cannot live

    without the danger

        of being this

utterly beautiful.

    And typical.

        And proven.

This continent: Fear—

    one's interior—

        uncharted

chaos—a nation

    modified—

        or suppressed

History trapped—

    in paralysis—unable

        to access weaknesses—

or strengths—and this: *We*

    are strongest—not for the Reason—

        but for the Record

most clearly revealed

    in the people. The war is

        a Lover's War.

And then the breast—
one blue quiet morning

(grey and neutral,
spotted and soft,

penetrable, mysterious,
steeled and velvet,

which is to say, black
and infinite—

in complete defiance of all
glacial desires, and

the World's relentless narration, Its own
wordless memorial—pulsing still)

nevertheless fills, protrudes—
and spreads—uncontrollably.

The deep center, first,
then the scalded chest.

My collar bones, next.
The body in revolt

again—again—against
its own (first) secret.

Without even wanting to, or
trying to, I lift my head—

red—and my new (again) hair. Red.
My red face returns. My red

skin. Red pores. Red bones.
All my atoms turn. Every cell

faces outward now. My red
beak. My red voice. Again

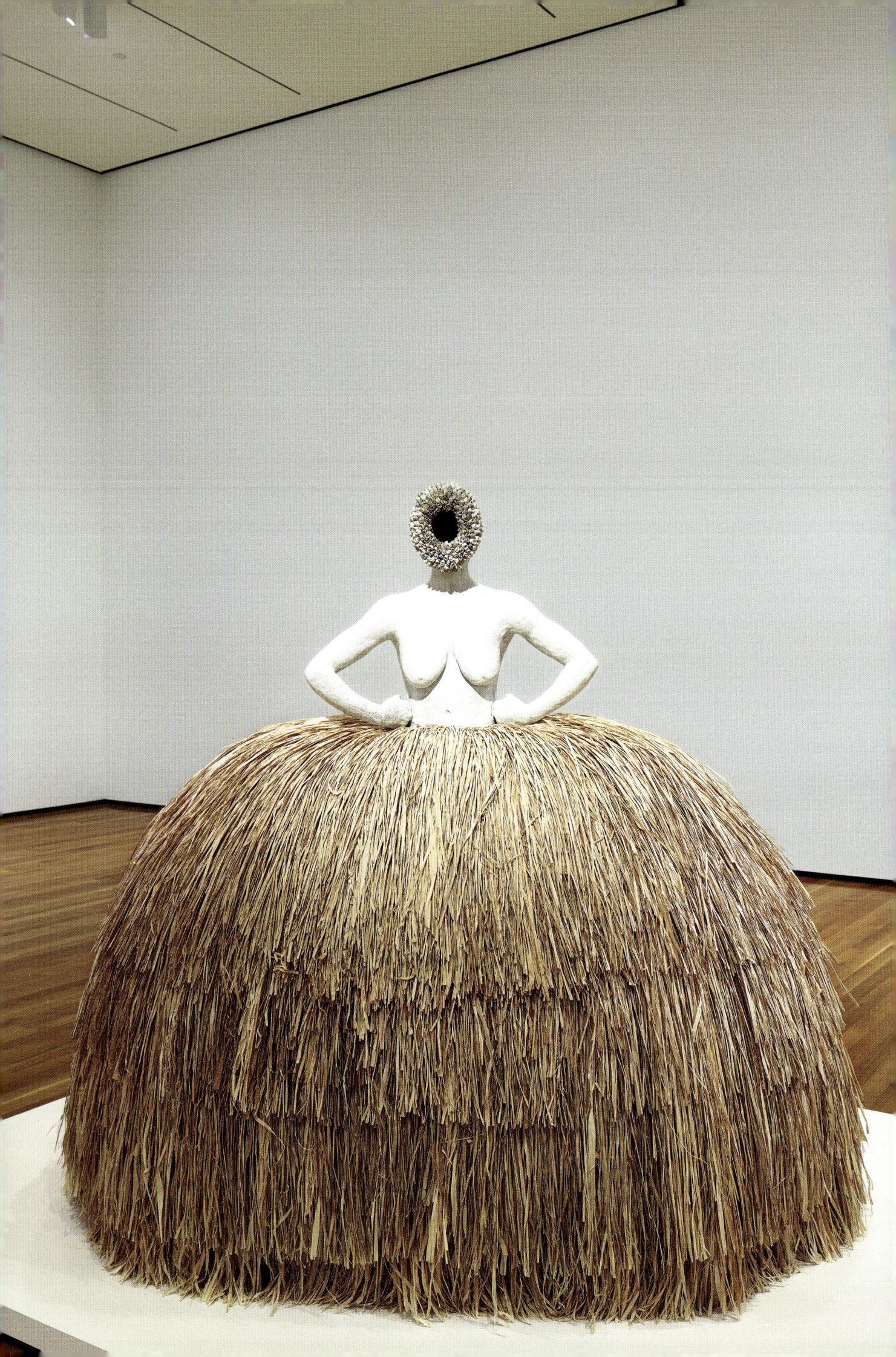

A GUST OF GRACE: SIMONE LEIGH'S *LAS MENINAS*
ERICA MOIAH JAMES

> *Colonialism is not satisfied merely with holding a people in its grip and emptying the native's brain of all form and content. By a kind of perverted logic, it turns to the past of oppressed people, and distorts, disfigures, and destroys it.*
>
> —Frantz Fanon[1]

> *How do you deal with the stereotyped view of yourself that you yourself have been socialized to accept? . . .*
>
> —Sylvia Wynter[2]

INTRODUCTION

Know that this is only part of the story. Narrative and meaning slip, slide, and change in fugitive art. And Simone Leigh's *Las Meninas* (2019) [fig. 31] is *necessarily* fugitive work. It is art that, in the words of Stuart Hall, "confront(s) the fragmented and pathological," art that "restore(s) an imaginary fullness or plenitude, set against the broken rubric of our past"—at least for a while.[3] This sculpture, a singular body with a title that suggests multiplicity, generates through materiality, form, and traces, the understanding that—once one sees and comes to *know* the frames that limit one's humanity in the face of colonial and psychic traumas—one must, as Sylvia Wynter insists, continue to take the risk of becoming.[4] This essay considers the ways in which Leigh's *Las Meninas* assembles Black diasporic imaginaries to map emancipatory histories and clear paths toward Black feminist futures.

I

In Hall's seminal series of televised lectures for the Open University, he spoke of circuits of meaning in art and the need to "perhaps learn to think of meaning less in terms of 'accuracy' and 'truth' and more in terms of effective change—a process of translation . . . which recognizes the persistence of *difference* and power."[5] *Difference* as described here cannot be captured in a binary because it is not a *something* that can be concluded. Instead, as Jacques Derrida posits, this difference describes a process, an evocation that is constantly being deferred, contested, and negotiated.[6] What might this mean for contemporary/Black/diasporic/women artists like Leigh who play with the unsettled character of difference and transform it into a point of departure in their work?

Leigh has been described as a ceramicist, a sculptor, an installation artist, and a master deployer of material and immaterial situational aesthetics. There is an ethical consciousness in her work that draws audiences in; a respectful, dare I say reverent, understanding of aesthetic practices—Black, "Western," and otherwise—that allows her seemingly enigmatic art to continually escape the grasp of indexicality. Leigh's work seeks understanding while presenting a pose of confident indifference. It occupies an unapologetic political space and insists that audiences look up to and/or face the figure directly, establishing the terms of engagement from the outset and in situ. This is art that invites audiences into a conversation but just as easily settles into opacities if they are not ready to do the work it demands.

In colonial societies (and here I use the term "colonial" to describe any organized act of oppression mobilized on a state level against a distinct group, rather than drawing on the temporal or cultural specificity of British colonialism), part of the anticolonial struggle is for colonized people to see themselves as they are rather than through the annihilating

FIGURE 31
Las Meninas, 2019. Simone Leigh (American, born 1967). Terracotta, steel, raffia, and porcelain; overall: 182.9 x 213.4 x 152.4 cm. The Cleveland Museum of Art, Purchased with funds donated by Scott Mueller, 2019.175. © Simone Leigh, courtesy the artist and Matthew Marks Gallery.

prism of the colonial gaze. "Anticolonial" does decolonial work. It can therefore be described as art that is auto-historiographic and nonlinear. It is art that mobilizes aesthetics to suture pasts to the present, recovering and rendering what appeared to be lost. The Cuban writer José Lezama Lima described it as art that in form and process simultaneously *critiques the past and creates with an eye on the future*; art that emerges in the wake of annihilating forces like "gusts of grace."[7] *Las Meninas*'s decolonial work enunciates from the vantage point of Black women. The sculpture appears fixed and immutable, but in the conceptual imaginary in which it operates it is fugitive and unstable in ways that give it life.

Leigh's fugitive art embodies a critical ethos found in Caribbean modernism that turns the aforementioned difference into dialogic différance, as described by Jacques Derrida and made plain by Hall. Hall describes the *A* in Derrida's spelling of *différance* as "a marker which sets up a disturbance in our settled understanding or translation of the shared word/concept. It sets the word in motion to new meanings without erasing the *trace* of its other meanings."[8] Here we might replace Hall's "word/concept" with "sculpture" and consider the ways the notion of *différance* more broadly sets Leigh's art in motion. It displaces and renders mute concepts of the Other by noting the ways in which these formerly othered artists draw many things into their work, inhabiting the spaces between binaries, embracing liminality and unsettled places that can be reimagined. The condition of *différance* in art objects is conceptual and immaterial. It recognizes that they are always emerging from past configurations—influences, references, histories—that leave traces and/or experiences within them. And yet the art irrefutably occupies a present, whole form and a signification accumulated through its material, composition, and temporal placement, signaling meaning that itself is both situated and in motion. The fugitive quality exhibited in this artwork can become labyrinthine, enabling it to escape into opacity in order to mount decolonial challenges to its theoretical and discursive calcification in an art world reductively obsessed with identity circa 1989. Teasing out several accumulated traces in *Las Meninas* points to the ways in which fugitive art extends signification, allowing the work to constantly become, to mourn, to laugh, to dance, and to glow.

II

Leigh's *Las Meninas* comprises the ceramic torso and head of a woman glazed in a dull white. What one reads as the figure's lower body consists of a large hoopskirt covered in raffia. Her face appears to be a void, encircled by a wreath of shell-like rosettes. She is less tall than she is wide, and her arms *appear to be* akimbo. Straight-backed and staring, despite the absence of literal eyes, the figure commands the space. It demands visibility—a *look-at-ness*. Even so, the work also pointedly resists a stable, closed reading. Every element produces multiple significations and contains multiple traces. Drawing on W. J. T. Mitchell's seminal work, *Las Meninas* can be seen as a super metaobject, one that endlessly multiplies in the conceptual plane. Mitchell describes "metapictures" as being "notoriously migratory, moving from popular culture to science, philosophy or art history, shifting from marginal positions as illustrations or ornaments to centrality and canonicity. They don't just illustrate theories of picturing and vision: they show us what vision is, and picture theory."[9] To admit that the work of non-white, non-male, "non-Western" artists possess this capacity as well opens the door to the decolonization of art history, and *Las Meninas* thus becomes both an artwork to regard and a theoretical form. To see this sculpture, then, not as a singular or linear event but as a way of being as much as seeing shakes away the ossified ways of engaging art that Mitchell posits were the standard before Michel Foucault's interdisciplinary engagement of seventeenth-century painter Diego Velázquez's *Las Meninas* (1656),[10] a clear reference for Leigh's sculpture.

Mitchell identifies the formal structure of Velázquez's painting as an "encyclopedic labyrinth of pictorial self-reference, representing the interplay between the beholder, the producer, and the object or model of representation as a complex cycle of exchanges and substitutions" and characterizes the work as "a comprehensive figure not only of a painterly style, but an episteme, an entire system of knowledge/power relations,"[11] qualities that can also be seen in Leigh's sculpture. If we think of a metaobject as the concretization of a process that is multiple and shifting across time, Leigh's *Las Meninas* is a labyrinthine metaobject in which African classical and Black diasporic elements become both formal components and historical avatars within a conceptually deployed episteme, resistant to concluded narratives. In process, the work's accumulation of traces makes its meaning productively unstable, and hence resists objectification as a fixed sign. By cultivating form within a multiplicity of traces, Leigh generates a condition of uncertainty for the work. The process of dissembling and dissemblance used to create this uncertainty can been seen as a sanctuary for the historically oppressed and marginalized. It allows the work to offer ongoing possibilities for self-fashioning in a liberated future, diffusing stereotypes and, in the process, neutering the power of the colonial gaze.

Mitchell posits that "metapictures elicit not just a double vision but a double voice, and a double relation between language and visual experience. . . . metapictures call into question the relation of language to image as an inside/outside structure."[12] This observation only hints at the prismatic nature of diasporic arts seen in Leigh's work. Today Mitchell's doubling is perhaps not enough to do the work it once could, but Leigh takes this as a starting point and amplifies it in the conceptual realm with *Las Meninas*'s *ibeji* twin, *No Face (Pannier)* (2018) [fig. 32]. Identical in shape, size, and form, its torso, in contrast, is glazed in a luminous raku black. In Yoruba cultures, the ultimate blessing is a twin birth. Ibeji twin sculptures are created to provide parents with a spiritual connection to twin children who do not survive childbirth. Leigh's two *Las Meninas* sculptures are intent on providing a similar connection for audiences. The figures first appear to materialize and suggest oppositions (black and white). However, extended engagement with them undercuts this first impression, revealing them to be far more discursive.

In "Living On—Border Lines" Derrida asks, "what are the borderlines of a text?"[13] Or, as we may apply this here, a work of art? How do they come about? What becomes possible at the edge of an object when one calls it "to appear"?[14] In its aggregate form *Las Meninas* sasses the assumption of order implied by binaries, opposites, fraternal twinning, yin and yang, and the scientific rule that for every action there is an equal and opposite reaction in the cultural economic and political spheres. What Leigh *calls to appear* through her work explodes easy assumptions of the canonical reference, asking those still dependent on organizational frameworks that find balance and order in binaries to double up multiple times and quicken the pace. In the contemporary art world, holding onto historically sanctioned rules of engagement based on narrow identity politics barely scratches the surface of intention and meaning in work being produced today. Such a lens remains on the edge, on the surface of the work. It is unable to see and plumb what has been called to appear.

When Leigh and artists like her create metaobjects like *Las Meninas*, these artworks embody knowledge and histories. And they draw on the performative to express the

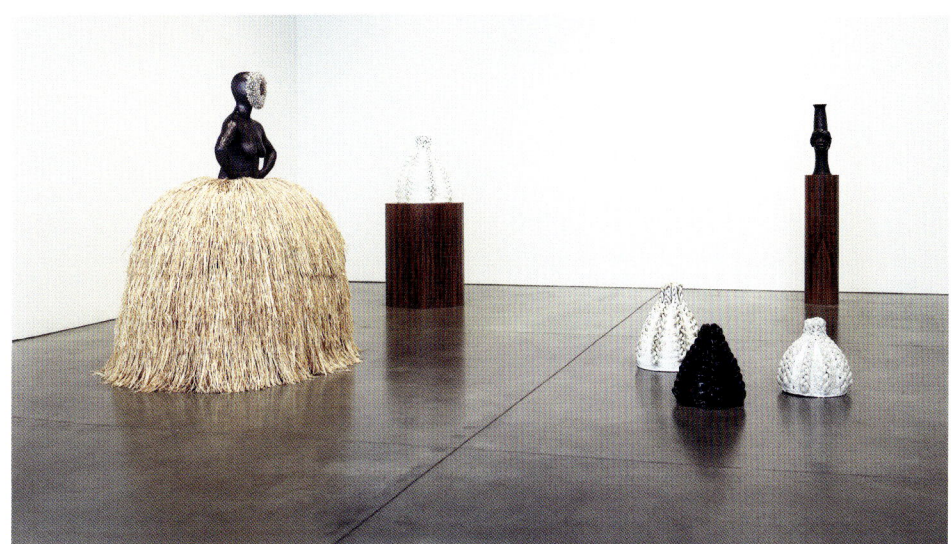

FIGURE 32
Installation view of **No Face (Pannier)**, 2018. Simone Leigh. © Simone Leigh, courtesy the artist and Matthew Marks Gallery.

rhizomatic experience of Black female being. It is difficult to settle on a unifying, singular sign or meaning in this work. The accumulation of traces suggests an ethos rather than a narrative. These traces make the quest for a single idea or the unification of signs in service to a stable narrative or meaning labyrinthine. In fugitive art like this, fracture, rhizomatic breaks, and labyrinths render spaces where Blackness can be, live, and remain generative. In fugitive art, meaning constantly shifts from plateau to plateau to ensure that the work does not become a fixed signifier and the referent body is not framed as Other. In fugitive art, the past and present comingle to create nonlinear approaches to history and discourse. Fugitive art does not "destroy structures from the outside," but instead can only "take accurate aim . . . by inhabiting those structures in *a certain way*." [15] This artwork demonstrates Derrida's paradigm of deconstruction, "operating necessarily from the inside, borrowing all the strategic and economic resources of subversion from the old structure, borrowing them structurally, that is to say without being able to isolate their elements and atoms, the enterprise of deconstruction always *in a certain way* falls prey to its own work."[16] As a fugitive work, Leigh's *Las Meninas* inhabits histories, discourses, cultures, and epistemes known in art history in order to *take accurate aim* and answer Wynter's decolonial question: It mobilizes traces to historically ground its contemporary strategy and critique in service to creation. It mobilizes traces in service to creation, grounding its contemporary strategy and critique in history.

III

Leigh's *Las Meninas* dances with history and signification by calling up and holding traces of cultural practices in its form. The artist has openly spoken of her interest in architecture, particularly Mousgoum architecture from Cameroon, elements of which she appropriates and transforms in her work. She was introduced to Mousgoum architecture and specifically the *teleuk* home through the work of Steven Nelson. In his careful study of the Mousgoum, Nelson examined the ways in which the form and images of the Mousgoum teleuk were reproduced and functioned within multiple discourses far beyond their point of creation.[17] For Nelson, the teleuk can be seen as a kind of living archive that documents the extraordinary design skills of a people and the equally extraordinary discursive life of this seemingly ordinary object. His approach to Mousgoum domestic architecture is the antithesis of typical visions of gendered home spaces seen in the American South, Victorian Britain, and, unsurprisingly, fascist Italy. This is decolonial art history that centers the ethos embedded in the form through trace. His method puts a punctum in Western ways of (un)seeing for Leigh to appropriate, absorb, reject, and transform in her practice.

The Mousgoum occupy an area in Northeast Cameroon that borders Chad. The beehive-shaped teleuk has come to express this culture's alignment with nature. Nelson describes it as an "environmentally friendly" building [fig. 33]. It "leaves no waste in its construction, and if it falls, the materials are completely biodegradable and totally reusable."[18] Knowing how this house lives in the culture that created it shapes an important thinking space. It makes clear that the form took shape within an aesthetic ethos in sync with the earth and its cycles, rather than in a colonial mindset of extraction and waste.

Like other cultures in Africa, the Mousgoum drew the teleuk form through the careful observation of their natural environment, specifically the ways ant and termite hills are constructed. As Nelson notes, teleuks reveal as much about the character of the Mousgoum as they do about those appropriating their form and ascribing new meanings to it in spaces outside of Cameroon through a process he describes as tectonics. Tectonics is "the mode through which construction becomes structure. It is the mechanism that transforms architecture into art. It is the device that . . . changes a 'hut' into a nearly perfect building. It is the method that allows us . . . to transcribe ourselves into architecture. As such, tectonics allows architecture to become not only a mirror but also a lens through which we see the world."[19] As Nelson, quoting American architectural theorist Detlef Mertins, elaborates, it bridges "the unbridgeable gap between self and other, known and unknown, conscious and unconscious in order to stabilize representations prone to coming apart."[20]

I quote Nelson at length because the idea expressed here congeals with those of Hall, Derrida, and Mitchell, as well as with the ways Leigh's contemporary art practice gathers the past through form to imagine new possibilities for our present. Leigh sometimes takes the teleuk form and reproduces in the bodies of her sculpture its beehive shape and structural elements that seemingly serve simultaneously as decoration. In *Brick House* (2016) [fig. 34], the literal reference riffs to perform tectonic work. One doesn't have to know the reference to appreciate the object, but to go beneath the surface of its

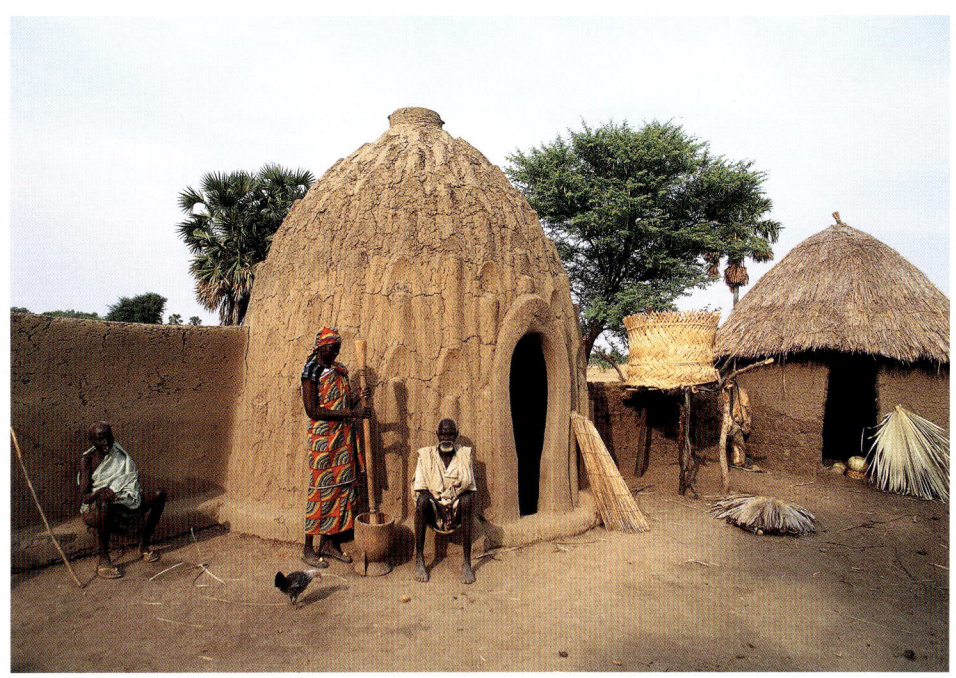

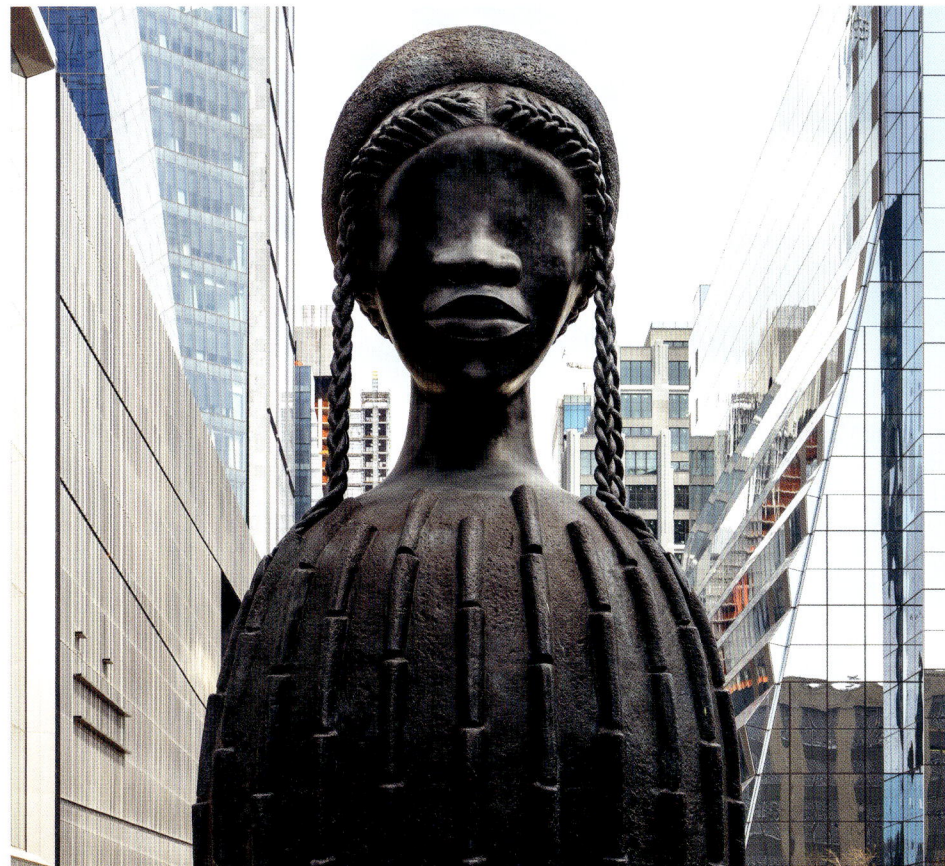

FIGURE 33
Mousgoum architecture. Photo: DeAgostini / Getty Images.

FIGURE 34
Brick House, 2019. Simone Leigh. A High Line Plinth commission. On view June 2019–May 2021. Artwork © Simone Leigh, courtesy the artist and Matthew Marks Gallery. Photo: Gerard Garcia.

representation impels one to learn more. Leigh's unambiguous contemporary appropriation and redeployment of the African vernacular enables these classic forms to reenter history and our present regard in new ways.

IV

The historical relationship between Leigh's *Las Meninas* and Velázsquez's eponymous canonical painting is another trace present in the sculpture. Created in 1656, Velázsquez's work [fig. 35a] is beguiling for many reasons, including how he presents the subject in space, extending the capacity of the frame and of one's experience of the composition into a conceptual plane. One does not merely look at this painting: audiences are quite literally a part of the work's spatial imaginary. The notion of subject and fixed understandings of subjectivity are both unmoored in this work, which provides a literal representational subject while conceptually rendering a "second subject" outside of the picture plane, in the space the viewer occupies. Rather than being a painting within a painting, as it is often described, it is a painting *in the world*. It does not rest on the wall but activates the space before it as an extension of its frame. It was a stunning work for the time and theorizes a formal aestheticization of gaze theory that collapse the hierarchies of vision and power—binary distinctions—in transformative ways. Leigh's sculpture similarly expands expectations of form and notions of appropriation and transformation across space and time.

There is not a single element of the painting that has not been pored over and detailed. However, recent scholarship has reconsidered a fascinating dimension that has special significance in the context of the feminist, Black Atlantic artistic practice that is Leigh's. In the lower center of the 1656 work a small tray is being presented to the Infanta Margaret Theresa, daughter of King Philip IV and Queen Mariana of Spain, who is dressed in the wide-skirted style of the day and stares intently out of the picture toward her parents and the viewer. On the tray is a small earthenware—specifically terracotta—vessel called a *búcaro* [fig. 35b]. Just behind the infanta, a red velvet pennant rests. Red curtains are also reflected in the mirror framing the presence of the king and queen. According to Byron Ellsworth Hamann,[21] the tray, búcaro, and curtains rendered Spain's "transatlantic connections." Imported from the "New World," they were produced through the "labor of Amerindian subjects of the Crown," meaning that all objects depicted by Velázquez in this painting were "made possible by Spain's colonial empire."[22]

The búcaro is of special note here. Hamann's exhaustive study marks it as having been produced in Guadalajara, Mexico.[23] In Spain, it was used exclusively to carry a substance known for its "mind- and body-altering qualities."[24] The clay was fired with a special blend of herbs that infused any water placed in it for the desired effect. Kelly Grovier notes that beyond drinking the steeped elixir, it became common practice for those in court circles to eat the búcaro bit by bit—amplifying the impact of the herbs on the mind and body, which as Grovier states had desired as well as unwanted consequences. Most important to the Spanish elite, "consuming this foreign clay" enabled "a

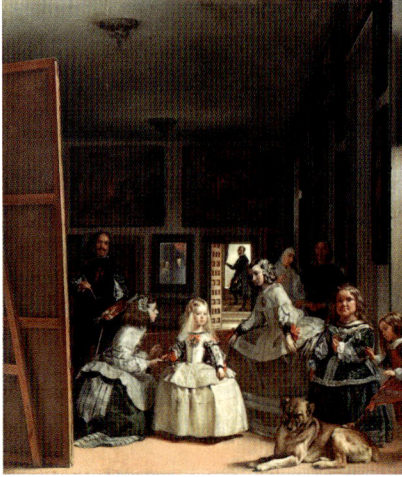
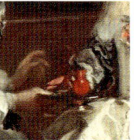

FIGURE 35a
Las Meninas, 1656.
Diego Velázquez (Spanish, 1599–1660). Oil on canvas; 320.5 x 281.5 cm. Museo Nacional del Prado, Madrid, P001174.

FIGURE 35b
Las Meninas
(detail), 1656.

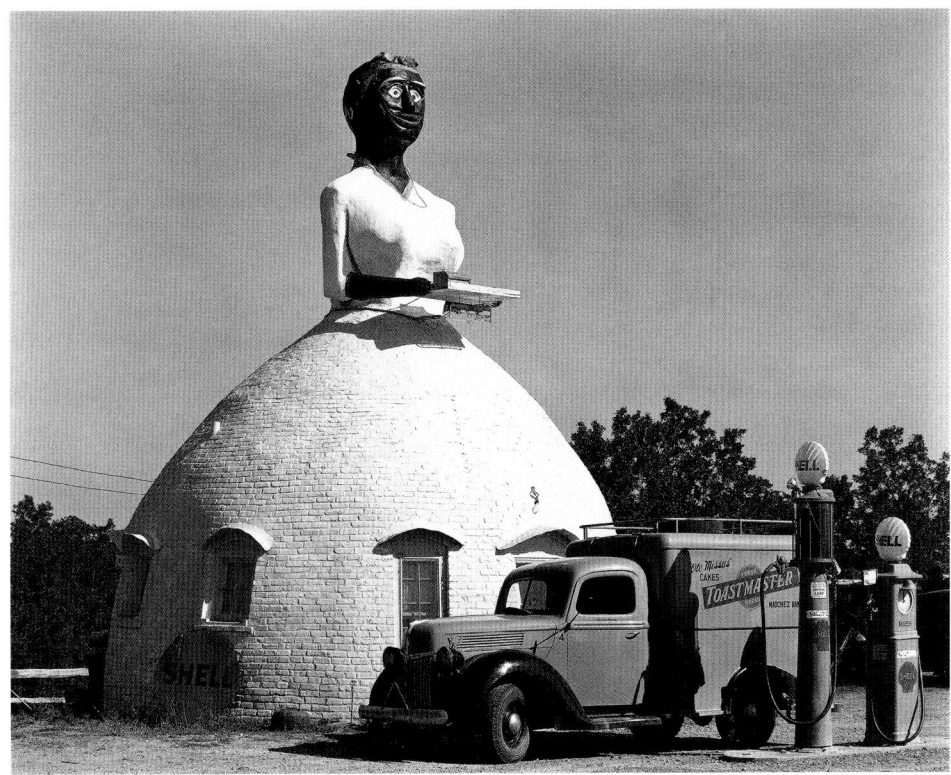

FIGURE 36
Mammy's Cupboard, Natchez, Mississippi, 1941. Edward Weston (American, 1886–1958). Gelatin silver print; sheet: 19.2 x 24.3 cm. Museum of Fine Arts, Boston, The Lane Collection, 2017.3532. Artwork © 2022 Center for Creative Photography, Arizona Board of Regents / Artists Rights Society (ARS), New York. Photo © 2022 Museum of Fine Arts, Boston.

dramatic lightening of the skin to an almost ethereal ghostliness."[25] This idea of skin lightening is not exclusive to any culture and has a long history from China to Jamaica, from the United States to South Africa. Although this practice is often critiqued today as a sign of colonial-determined racial self-hatred when considered in relation to non-white users, Velázquez's *Las Meninas* (1656) reminds us that even "white" people actively pursue the imagined ideal of literally white skin. No one is exempt from the totality of whiteness. We are all caught in this skewed concept of beauty in a color hierarchy that continually feeds established assumptions based on skin color and class, often with devastating results. As with all uses of narcotics, consuming a búcaro in pursuit of whiteness came with severe consequences. Its use could destroy the liver, consume red blood cells that were not being replaced quickly enough, and cause paralysis and hallucinations.[26] In the minds of Europeans however, these risks were far outweighed by the benefits of luminous whiteness.

With each of the objects it depicts, the painting marks itself as being part of a global circuit of commerce and exchange. It also historicizes the formal investment in the literal production of whiteness from the highest echelons of European society, achieved—not without irony—by their extraction and ingestion of a product produced in the Americas by non-white persons. Like the architecture described by Nelson and Mertins, *Las Meninas* thus becomes *not only a mirror but also a lens through which we see the world*, and bridges *the unbridgeable gap between self and other, known and unknown, conscious and unconscious*. The same holds true from multiple vantage points for works like Leigh's *Las Meninas*.

V

Chloe Wyma, writing of Leigh's *Cupboard VIII* (2018) in a review for *Artforum*, notes how the sculpture, one of a series of related works that would later include *Las Meninas*, echoed the form of Mammy's Cupboard, a diner along Highway 61 in Natchez, Mississippi, built in the form of a stereotypical Black Mammy figure and made famous in a photograph taken by Edward Weston in 1941 [fig. 36].[27] Although the diner has been repainted countless times since it was photographed by Weston, in an effort, one now presumes, to rid the site of its unsavory relationship to slavery and Black stereotypes (the figure is currently painted in pinkish flesh tones), Weston's image reveals the roots of its making. Leigh's *Las Meninas* is conceptually tied to Natchez as much as it is to Madrid

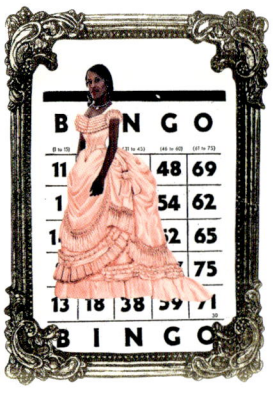 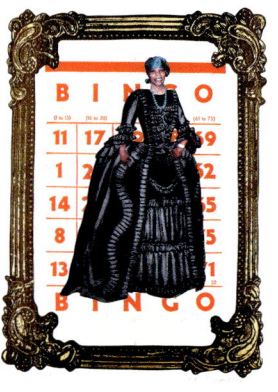 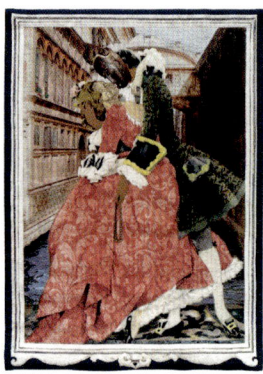

FIGURE 37a
I've been a Witness to this Game XV, 2016. Mildred Howard (American, born 1945). Digital monoprint on found paper with collage and metal leaf; 51.1 x 38.4 cm. Collection of the Jordan Schnitzer Family Foundation. © Mildred Howard. Photo: Bud Shark.

FIGURE 37b
I've been a Witness to this Game XVIII, 2016. Mildred Howard. Digital monoprint on found paper with collage and metal leaf; 51.1 x 38.4 cm. © Mildred Howard 2016. Photo: Bud Shark.

FIGURE 37c
Casanova: Style, Swagger, and the Embracement of the Other—I, 2018. Mildred Howard. Jacquard tapestry; 182.9 x 137.2 cm. © Mildred Howard. Images courtesy Mildred Howard and Magnolia Editions.

and Cameroon. The ever-expanding prism of relationships exhibited in the form as traces crafts a complicated, atemporal, multidirectional system of interconnected physical, cultural, and discursive spaces often thought of as being independent of each other to reveal, as Lisa Lowe has argued, the intimacies of four continents.[28]

Mammy's Cupboard takes the form of a full-skirted, stereotypical mammy figure, tray in hands, unmediated Black skin, head tie, full red lips and cheeks, and wide bright eyes, all masked with an impossibly bright fixed smile. Her skirt area comprises the main space of the diner, the place where Southern white patrons came to eat from the time the restaurant was built in 1939–40. Travel writers have researched the history of the space, the owners, designers, and reasons behind the skirt form, which might just as easily have indicated that the structure was initially intended to represent a white Southern belle. However, the presence of the tray in hand suggests otherwise, and whatever the intention may have been does not blunt what it became—an object so deliberate that it affirms intention through form. Recalling Nelson's concept of tectonics, and Mertins's sense of the ways architecture bridges *the unbridgeable gap between self and other, known and unknown, conscious and unconscious in order to stabilize representations prone to coming apart*, I am interested in the skirt as architecture and the ways its form is imbricated with histories of Black female life that appear as shadow dance and trace in Leigh's *Las Meninas*. In Mammy's Cupboard, this eternally happy Black female figure has been monumentalized. But in the deepest of ironies, people enter or go under her skirt "to eat" every day all day. She has no choice in the matter. One doubts that Mammy's Cupboard would have appeared in the Green Book as a safe space for Black travelers to dine. Its form, era, and placement in Natchez would have marked its early audience as *white only*. With its broad, accessible petticoats, Mammy's Cupboard was/is a revelatory tectonic Freudian slip for its intended patrons.

In her seminal study on the Mammy/Jezebel dynamic in American history, Deborah Gray White historicizes the Mammy and Jezebel figures in mythologies of Black female slavery and more precisely white narratives of Southern slavery where Black women are simultaneously characterized as "infantile, irresponsible, submissive and promiscuous."[29] Living at the interstices of subjugation due to her race and gender, the Black woman, White argues, "gains none of the deference and approbation that accrue from being perceived as weak and submissive" (she can have no expectation of the grace afforded white women, however problematic the terms), and she cannot claim any "advantages that come with being a white male."[30] White continues, "To be so 'free,' in fact, has at times made her appear to be a superwoman, and she has attracted the envy of black males and white females. Being thus exposed to their envy she has often become their victim."[31] This is conceptually rendered in Leigh's *Las Meninas* through the trace of Mammy's Cupboard in the work.

Where enslaved Black and mixed-race women appear in archives and literature, they are often described as simultaneously unattractive, animal-like, naturally sensual, and lascivious. The Jezebel version of this figure was prone to tempting white slave owners into sexual relations, trying to displace the white "mistress," using her body to ingratiate herself with white male power, and feeling honored at having brought a mixed-race child into the world. The undying lie of the Mammy/Jezebel matrix during this period and into today is a central topic of Mildred Howard's series *I've Been a Witness to this Game* (2016) [fig. 37a,b]. Here Howard collages Black women into period dress in the design language used for the covers of historical romance novels. She amps up the intense manufactured emotions such novels generate in works such as *Casanova: Style, Swagger, and the Embracement of the Other I* (2019) [fig. 37c]. In Howard's collages, the critical subjects are rendered through a representational mode that also recalls paper dolls, alluding to construction, fantasy, and dishonesty in the creation of these tropes.

Acknowledgment and critique of the Mammy/Jezebel stereotype are embedded in the accumulated traces Leigh's sculpture carries. The narcissism that slavery cultivated meant that the slave status of the Black woman and the meting of sexual and physical violence upon her were her fault alone. The immorality of white male slavers and their aggrieved wives was projected onto the body of the enslaved Black woman. If we think of the experience of Patsey, the young woman who lived on the plantation where Solomon Northrup was enslaved, desire comingled with rape and the physical violence of endless beatings. In the wounds of Patsey's flesh, the myth of Jezebel congealed. In this system of signification, the Mammy [fig. 38], presented here as a cookie jar, can be seen as a mythical corrective in defense of slavery. Gray White makes the binary clear: "One was carnal, the other maternal. One was at heart a slut, the other was deeply religious. One was a Jezebel, the other a Mammy."[32]

Relying on White, broadly speaking, if Jezebel was a wanton mistress, Mammy "was a woman completely dedicated to the white family, especially to the children of that family. She was the house servant who was given complete charge of domestic management. She served also as a friend and advisor. She was, in short, surrogate mistress and mother."[33] She was not on paper a rival to the white mistress of her household. Her unmitigated Blackness, excessive weight, and age made her theoretically the antithesis of desire—ha. However, spaces like Mammy's Cupboard and collectibles such as the Mammy Cookie Jar tectonically reveal that assumptions about Mammy's asexual nature and undesirability were lies.

In fact, the Mammy can be seen as America's own Georgian redux, without the pictorial intimacy of Georgian art. In the United States, white representations of Black bodies emphasized a *blessed violence*—increasingly seen in the ritualization of free access to commoditized, intimately handled, casually violated, and, in some cases, symbolically sexually violated cookie jars, banks, etc., as stand-ins for Black, often female, bodies. Mammy's Cupboard concretizes dynamics of race and gender in America while allowing everyone who enters its doors to participate in the passive violation of Black women by proxy. As a metaobject Leigh's work carries and critiques this violent history lest we forget it. However, refusing to be ensnared, her *Las Meninas* transcends it all.

VI

To speak of Leigh's *Las Meninas* as a Black woman may appear to be to disregard the literal whiteness of the sculpture's bare-breasted torso. But recalling Ferdinand de Saussure, if Blackness is not literal, the same holds true for whiteness.[34] To see the figure's skin literally and in relation to its darker twin sister invites reflection on the

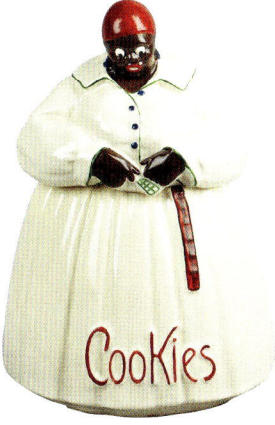
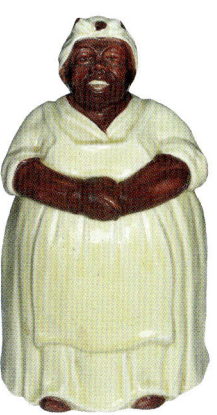

FIGURE 38
Aunt Jemima cookie jars.
Photos via Google Images.

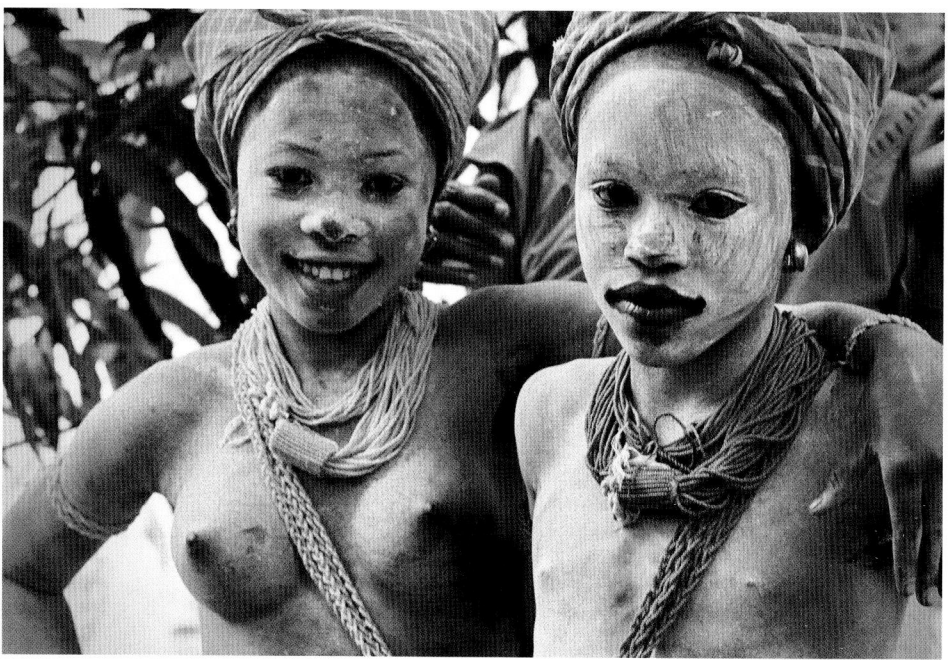

possibility of allyship among women across races. It can also be seen as a universal synecdoche for the full range of women the sculpture's name references, or conversely as a critique of cultural appropriation. But other traces in the work complicate matters. In *Las Meninas* at least two West African performance traditions that center Black women are also present: the Sande Society of Sierra Leone, Liberia, and neighboring countries, and the Great Nimba Mask danced by the Baga people of Guinea.

Sylvia Ardyn Boone and Ruth B. Phillips have completed seminal research on Mende art and traditions. Boone focused her core research on the Sande Society, the only known masking tradition exclusively for African women, danced by women. Following the work of Walter Rodney and his landmark study *History of the Upper Guinea Coast: 1545–1800*, Boone described the Society as an "international," "multi-ethnic," "numerically immense" organization centered on the protection, care, and support of Black women.[35] The society attracts large numbers of women from throughout West Africa and the international diaspora. It has also had a major impact on the politics of West African nations. When the Sande Society's signature Bundu mask is fully finished and danced, Boone argues that "the spirit of Sande, the concrete materialization of the society's precepts and ideals" are being communicated.[36] Everything created and utilized by the society carries meaning, sometimes multiple meanings, and the Bundu mask can also be seen as a kind of protective talisman, capable of standing against anything that creates difficulties or seeks to harm a Sande member.

The aesthetics of the Bundu mask and the way of the dance communicate the society's emphasis on deportment as well as its mission to cultivate and value women who are smart, refined, and aware of their responsibilities as women. But in the context of Leigh's *Las Meninas* I want to emphasize the importance of whitening the bodies of young women during their initiation into the Sande Society and how it may necessitate a more nuanced reading of whiteness in relation to this sculpture.

The signification of whiteness has been colonized in modernity as a synecdoche for people of European descent. By embodying traces of the Sande Society and the meaning of whiteness in various African cultural contexts, Leigh's work untangles this embrace of whiteness as a fixed sign. *Las Meninas* appears chalky rather than smooth; a dull, literal white that lacks the luminosity of skin. It is a signifying whiteness rather than a literal one.

To prepare for their time away from their families and to signal the beginning of the initiation process, Mende girls gather on the appointed day and are greeted with embraces and celebration by the older Sande initiates. The girls' clothes are removed, and their

FIGURE 39
Young Mende Initiates.
Sowei Society. Photo
© Rebecca Busselle.

entire bodies are covered in a white porcelain kaolin clay called *hojo* [fig. 39]. This clay is used in a variety of circumstances by the society to, in every sense, claim the person, place, or thing it marks as belonging to the Sande or being Sande. It marks boundaries and declares ownership. There is no trespassing on a body under hojo. It boldly declares of the initiates/*mbogboni*: "She is ours."[37] The young girl enters her initiation as a girl covered in hojo and returns to her family as a woman in her natural skin.

Think about this deployment of whiteness in relation to Velázquez's *Las Meninas* and the desired effects of the búcaro infusion on the skin. In 1656, the year Velázquez's painting was completed, the Spanish elite lightened their skin to provide evidence of the mythologies of difference created around whiteness. Among the Sande, whiteness is deployed conceptually to express a process of transformation. In one culture, whiteness is pursued ontologically at the risk of life itself; in the other, it represents a condition to be passed through, signifying maturity and the ability of the former initiate to now create life.

Boone affirms that it is the characteristics of the material rather than its literal whiteness that are of utmost importance and value for the Sande.[38] Hojo's moist, cool qualities are akin to youthfulness. Its smooth, glossy, shiny surface exhibits luminosity once fired and speaks symbolically to the initiation process as a kind of literal firing process for these young women, who will be transformed into luminous Sande Women, prepared for marriage. Hojo also comes from the waters and is therefore aligned with primordial animals that survive in land and water, as well as with Yemaya/Yemoja, the goddess of the waters in Yoruba and Kongo belief systems, whose liturgic colors are blue and white. According to Boone, the varying shades of white hojo exhibits communicate how deep the women went into the riverbank to obtain it. With the most luminous clays only available at great depths, acquiring the lightest hojo suggests perseverance—a positive trait among Sande women.

As in other African cultures, such as the Baule and the Punu, and as seen in this extraordinary Punu reliquary figure from Gabon [fig. 40], white is a color that also symbolizes the mystical, the spirit world, an in-between space.[39] It is also a sign of things valued by the Sande, such as cleanliness, purity, spirits and ancestors, cleared spaces, freedom from encumbrances, transparency, visibility, luminosity, impartiality, fairness, clear thought, and justice. And it is symbolic of the light Sande are said to bring to a community

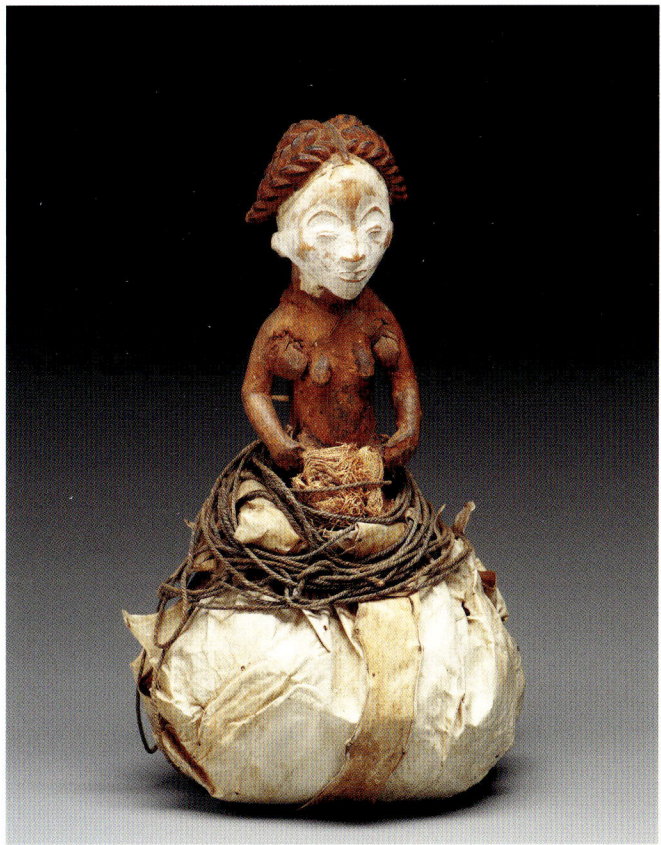

FIGURE 40
Protective statuette, related to divinatory practices, 19th c. Punu populations, Lumbo, Gabon. Wood, vegetable fiber, kaolin, and sacrificial matter; 32 x 18 x 18 cm. Musée du Quai Branly—Jacques Chirac, Paris, 71.1943.0.433. Photo: Musée du Quai Branly—Jacques Chirac. Dist. RMN-Grand Palais / Valerie Torre / Art Resource, New York.

they enter or occupy. These are not characteristics encoded onto human beings that refer to themselves as white. Here white is not racially inscribed. It is a condition or character anyone can assume. The Sande conceptualize white in ways detached from bodies, allowing Leigh's whitened figure be read as culturally African or Black while occupying a kind of liminal space or existence pictured as white. As stated above, once the Sande initiate has come through the process, she emerges with the physical qualities desired by Sande women and expressed in the Bundu mask—dark, smooth, flawless skin.

As seen in the Mousgoum teleuk, clay is fundamental to the making of homes and vessels across the continent—objects that cover and protect and objects that carry and transfer. Here the hojo clay spiritually connects each young girl with the rhythms of the earth and the circle of life. She has been symbolically transformed into a vessel. Leigh's use of whiteness as surface and sign in this work objectifies and destabilizes it, treating it like an element that can be re-signified as needed. In the artist's hands, white is a color.

The extended signification exhibited in the white torso of Leigh's *Las Meninas* is repeated in her monumental redeployment of *raffir*, a material indelibly associated with performance traditions from the Guru and Egjaham peoples of West Africa to Junkanoo and carnival players in the Caribbean. Like clay, it too has been used widely in architectural forms throughout Africa and its diaspora for hundreds of years. The skirt forms seen in *Las Meninas* and *Cupboard IV* resonate with the Mousgoum and with Nelson's concept of tectonic signification. Leigh's consideration of these sculptures as home spaces, worship spaces, palaces, vessels, etc., extends to their signifying capacity to shelter, to protect, to comfort, to provide rest. The material and form have extraordinary range in the African diaspora across time. The raffir dome as a structure comprised Fon royal *djehos* (houses for the soul) in Benin during the eighteenth and nineteenth centuries [fig. 41a]. It was the structure of mosques in the Fouta Djallon until the mid-twentieth century [fig. 41b]. It can be seen transported to the Caribbean in early homes Africans were forced to build for themselves on the island of St. Kitts [fig. 41d] and it is still the basis of contemporary architecture as seen in Dorze villages and houses in Southern Ethiopia [fig. 41c].

FIGURE 41a
A royal *djeho*, c. 1874. Fon, Benin. Finials represent *fa* image of deceased leader. Photo via Google Images.

FIGURE 41b
Great Mosque. Fouta Djallon, Guinea. Photographed c. 1940. © Michel Huet / GAMMA RAPHO

FIGURE 41c
Dorze House. Ethiopia. Photo: Alexander Ludwig / Alamy.

FIGURE 41d
Painting of Brimstone Hill, c. 1975. Attributed to Lt. James Lees. Courtesy the St. Kitts Archives, St. Kitts, West Indies.

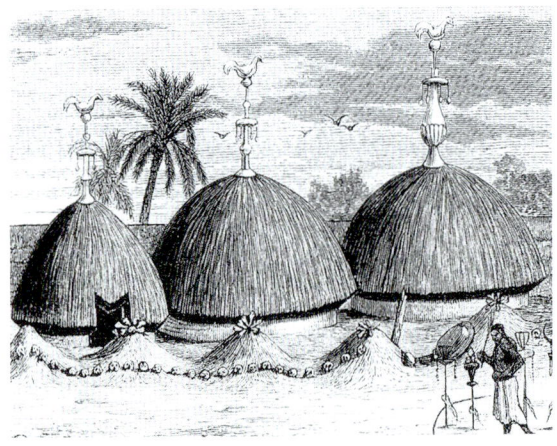
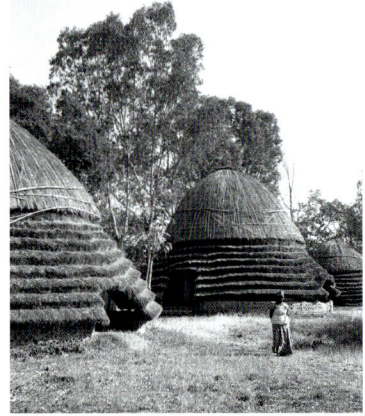
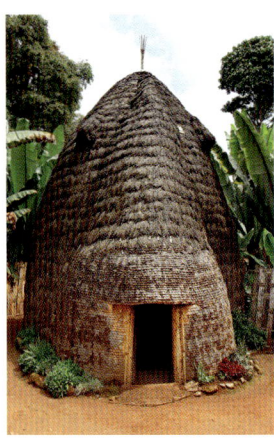
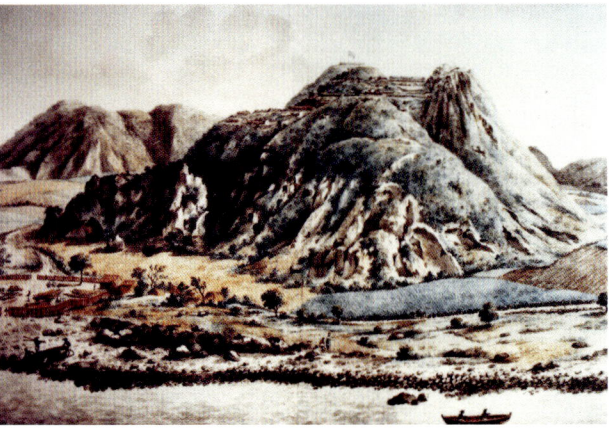

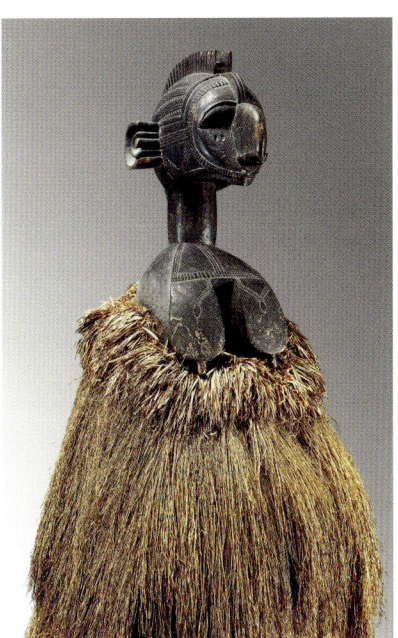
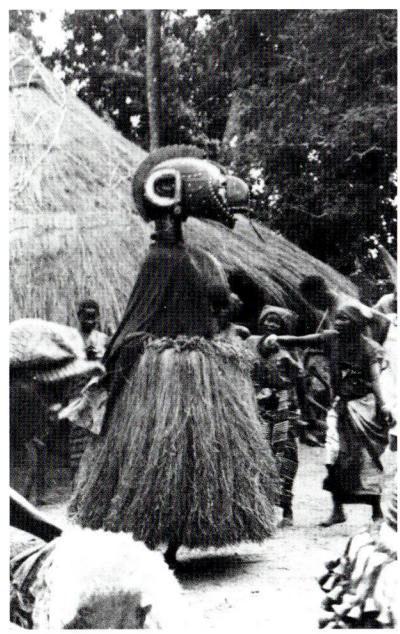

FIGURE 42a
Nimba shoulder mask. African, Baga. Wood and vegetable fiber. Musée du Quai Branly—Jacques Chirac, Paris. Photo: Musée du Quai Branly—Jacques Chirac, Dist. RMN-Grand Palais / Art Resource, New York.

FIGURE 42b
Nimba dance, c. 1940. Béatrice Appia (French, 1899–1998). Digital scan of a nitrate negative; 9 x 12 cm. Musée du Quai Branly—Jacques Chirac, Paris. © Estate of Béatrice Appia. Photo: Musée du Quai Branly—Jacques Chirac, Dist. RMN-Grand Palais / Art Resource, New York.

It can be said that Leigh's maids carry their homes with them/in them, as Africans have done for centuries no matter the circumstances. Rather than referencing the transatlantic slave trade as the tabula rasa it was once thought to be, *Las Meninas* continually points toward different imaginaries, an accumulation of things once thought lost.

Leigh's use of voluminous raffir also recalls the Ancient Mother of the Baga people of Guinea, who takes form in the Nimba Mask [fig. 42a]. The Baga people found themselves in the cross hairs of Marxism, Islam, and disenchantment in the years leading up to and after Guinea gained independence from France in 1958. Their story provides a sound warning about equating the concept and temporal implications of the postcolonial with anti- or decolonial action. Frederick Lamp describes how during the lead-up to independence, Baga faiths and cultural traditions were deemed backward by the Marxist leaders who would soon govern an independent Guinea. At the same time, Islam was spreading quickly, and young people were increasingly vocal regarding their lack of opportunity.[40] As a result, many of the objects associated with Baga ritual were caught in a perfect storm. The government, Muslims, and the disenchanted all wanted them gone. They were seized, exported, or destroyed by the government in a stated effort to modernize the people of Guinea and satisfy various ideologies and factions.[41]

An eradication movement influenced by religion, ideology, and disenchantment and led by men: There is much to consider regarding why certain objects were deemed particularly primitive and backward as part of this effort, but one of the main works targeted at the time was the Ancient Mother Mask, the Nimba or D'imba Mask [fig. 42b]. One of the largest in all of Africa, it required a man that possessed a great deal of strength and skill to dance. Scholarship conducted by Lorraine Bangoura not long after the mask was outlawed notes that:

> The Nimba is the principal work of art of the Baga people. . . . The mask is about two meters high but is very massive, weighing about thirty to forty-five kilos. It has a human head with jutting eagle-like nose. The expression is rather blank, but not grotesque. The mask includes a bust. On the day appointed, Nimba appears on the shoulders of its very strong carrier, who is hidden by a long fiber (raffir) cape.[42]

Before the ritual was outlawed, the Nimba mask was danced before the harvest as a sign of fertility and abundance. The Ancient Mother it embodied was seen as a transformative figure, formally expressed in her part bird, part human form.

Following his fieldwork in Guinea in the 1980s, almost thirty years after the last Nimba had been danced, Lamp rejected the belief that the Great Mother was a "goddess of fecundity," as described in earlier scholarship. Instead, he proposed that "she represents simply the idea of a woman who has borne children," and that the Baga he met "insist that she is not even of the status of a spirit (wi-kärfin)."[43] However, as Lamp would later reflect, when he conducted his fieldwork, few Baga alive remembered the ritual in total or the object's full significance because of government oppression. He noted too the extraordinary efforts the Baga made to recover what had been lost when laws banning the traditions loosened. He also conceded that the Nimba's size, her place as a shrine object, and the importance of her veneration among the Baga at a key time for the population seem to suggest a level of importance unlike no other. For this culture, the continued life and prosperity of their community was not affirmed until this figure entered the ritual space. Her spent breasts indicated that she had borne and nursed children, that she was fertile, and that her blessing would transfer to the land, producing rich harvests. Before the destruction, her veneration was considered of utmost importance in celebrating and promoting both human and agricultural fertility and growth.[44] While one can only speculate as to why this mask received special attention for destruction, for *Las Meninas* to call up this tradition as trace further expands the historical dimensions of this contemporary work and its ethical intent. By echoing this venerated, debased, and revived form, *Las Meninas* reminds audiences of the need to go fetch the past and begin anew in the wake of colonial destruction, while simultaneously affirming community care of Black women and the necessity of recognizing, honoring, and protecting the work they do to sustain themselves and communities they occupy.

VII

One of the most striking aspects of Leigh's *Las Meninas* is its "face," a void framed by a wreath of rosettes. Sonia Boyce's painting *She Ain't Holding Them Up, She's Holding On (Some English Rose)* (1986), reminds us of the fraught relationship Black women have had with the racialized feminine interpretations of the rose. Roses have extensive

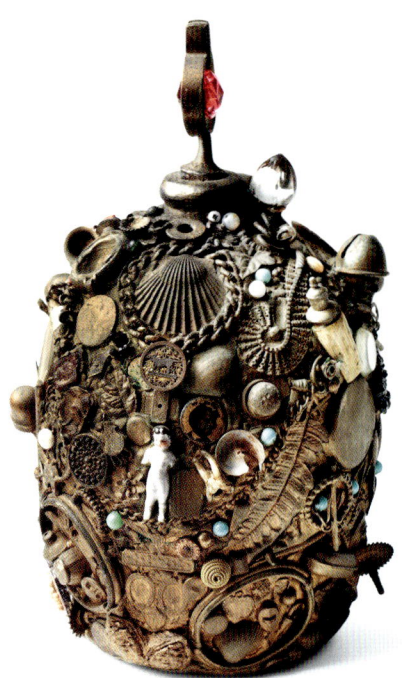

FIGURE 43
Memory jug with finial, 1900s. Maker unidentified. Mixed media on ceramic; 29.8 x 19.1 x 18.4 cm. Smithsonian American Art Museum, Gift of Herbert Waide Hemphill, Jr. and museum purchase made possible by Ralph Cross Johnson, 1986.65.310.

significance in global cultures. As with the "English Rose" they often signified something to be cherished and adored. Roses are so much a part of contemporary life that their significations are commonly known. Red roses signify romantic, passionate love; yellow mean friendship and warmth. White roses can be a sign of mourning, innocence, hope, or rebirth. Lavender are for adoration and love. The term "sub-rosa" (under the rose) originally meant that anything said in a space sanctioned by the presence of a bunch of the delicate flowers was confidential. Here in Leigh's work, an untold number of roses, in a range of white hues, from gray-white to a yellow-tinged bright white, frame the figure's face. On close examination even the interior of the facial void is covered in small roses.

They are not presented to her as a gift or worn by her as a sign of accomplishment; they are a part of her. The reverence signified by the rose and the Nimba is now boldly claimed within Leigh's Black female body.

Several years ago, I was in Jamaica to jury a summer biennial. While there I had a fascinating after-hours conversation with the National Gallery of Jamaica's staff on the role of literalness in Jamaican and Caribbean art. Rather than dismissing the practice as one-dimensional, the group saw it in part as a necessary overture, a trust bridge that when done well can transport the work and its audiences into an experience full of surprises. I am reminded of that conversation when I look at Leigh's work because there is a similar ethos brewing. Each element of her *Las Meninas* is recognizable—known in a certain way, a literal way, in relation to each other and in the context of the whole—but just as one recognizes this, first readings of the work enact fugitivity and begin to dissemble

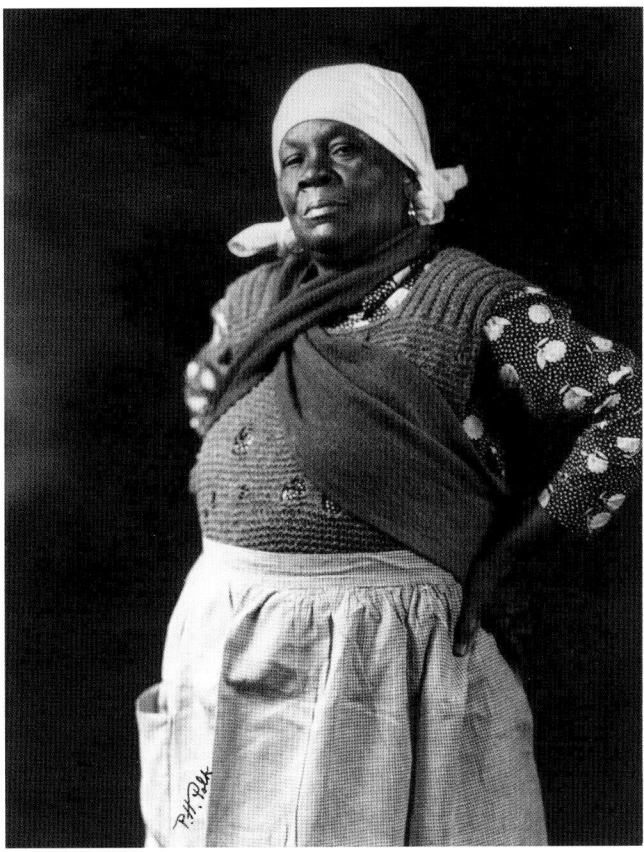

and fracture in time and space, calling up the traces of the Black past to write a history of our present anew. *Las Meninas* thus functions conceptually in ways similar to a memory jug [fig. 43]. Cobbled from objects of specific meaning to a Black person's life in the South, gathered together in a single clay vessel, memory jugs can be seen as a literal interpretation of the ways Leigh brings together various traces of the transatlantic universe in a single form, where meaning shifts according to endless configurations as traces rise. There is no Black life outside of history here. The story isn't one of abjection but of endless re-memory of the bitter and rebirth of the sweet, even if that means giving birth to oneself.

FIGURE 44
The Boss, 1932. Prentiss H. Polk (American, 1898–1984). Gelatin silver print; 24.1 x 18.7 cm. Detroit Institute of Arts, Gift of Delano Willis, F1988.119. Image courtesy of the Detroit Institute of Arts. © The Tuskeegee University Archives, Tuskeegee University.

VIII

On a first encounter with *Las Meninas*, the figure initially appears to have her arms akimbo, in the manner of Prentiss H. Polk's *The Boss* (1932), with all the dignity and strength expressed in that figure's carriage and gaze [fig. 44]. But as one looks closer and moves around it in space, the sculpture begins to suggest otherwise. The pose becomes increasingly unnatural and no longer registers as a defiant stance. Instead, what one begins to sense is a body on the cusp of movement, a specific dance movement I recalled through muscle memory.

In African dance classes, one of the first moves taught is the one expressed in *Las Meninas*: Arms bowed to the sides. Elbows slightly forward. Hands balled at the waist. Dancers stand shoulder to shoulder in a straight line facing in the direction they will move. When prompted, they jump in rhythm from one foot to the other, arms fluttering back and forth, gliding across the room in a manner similar to the Ghanaian Agbadza dance. Before this sculpture, the memory of performing this movement so many times took over and I could no longer see the figure standing still, arms akimbo in the gallery, holding court. Instead, the energy shifted, affirming once more this work's fugitive nature. As a metaobject, it gathers in its form traces of the distortion, disfigurement, violence, and destruction visited on Black women and Black people, but it also evokes psychic reassembly, self-fashioning, and self-care to affirm something new: the moment on the edge of a new beginning. This single form embodies a multitude, waiting for the drum to begin. Then, with its raffir skirt responding to every move, it will dance, each gesture affirming Black life, narrating Black pasts, registering Black creativity, marking history and entering a liberated future in a gust of grace.

1. Frantz Fanon, "On National Culture," in *The Wretched of the Earth*, preface by Jean-Paul Sartre (New York: Grove Press, 1963), 210.

2. Sylvia Wynter, in David Scott, "The Re-enchantment of Humanism: An Interview with Sylvia Wynter," *Small Axe* 8 (September 2000): 131, 134.

3. Stuart Hall, "Cultural Identity and Cinematic Representation," in *Diaspora and Visual Culture: Representing Africans and Jews,* ed. Nicholas Mirzoeff (New York: Routledge, 1989), 23.

4. Wynter, 139.

5. Stuart Hall, "The Work of Representation," in *Representation: Cultural Representations and Signifying Practices*, ed. Hall (London: Sage Publications, 1997), 10–11.

6. Ibid., 42.

7. José Lezama Lima, "Julián del Casal," translated by Robin Myers, *Small Axe* 23, no. 3 (November 2019): 133.

8. Stuart Hall, "Cultural Identity and Diaspora," in *Diaspora and Visual Culture*, ed. Mirzoeff, 26.

9. W. J. T. Mitchell, "Metapictures," in *Picture Theory: Essays on Verbal and Visual Representation* (London and Chicago: University of Chicago Press, 1994), 57.

10. Michel Foucault, "Las Meninas," in *The Order of Things: An Archaeology of the Human Sciences* (New York: Vintage, 1994), 3–16. (Originally published in France as *Les Mots et les choses* by Editions Gallimard, in 1966, and in English by Pantheon Books, in 1971.)

11. Mitchell, "Metapictures," 58.

12. Ibid., 68.

13. Jacques Derrida, "Living On—Border Lines," in *A Derrida Reader: Between the Blinds*, ed. Peggy Kamuf (New York: Columbia University Press, 1991), 258.

14. Ibid.

15. Derrida, "Of Grammatology," in *A Derrida Reader,* 41.

16. Ibid.

17. See Steven Nelson, *From Cameroon to Paris: Mousgoum Architecture In and Out of Africa* (London and Chicago: University of Chicago Press, 2007).

18. Ibid., 2.

19. Ibid., 5–6.

20. Ibid., 6.

21. See Byron Ellsworth Hamann, "Interventions: The Mirrors of Las Meninas: Cochineal, Silver, and Clay," *Art Bulletin* 92, no. 1–2 (2010): 6–35.

22. Ibid.,15.

23. Ibid., 1, 15–17.

24. Kelly Grovier, "Velázquez's *Las Meninas*: A Detail that Decodes a Masterpiece," BBC, October 16, 2020, https://www.bbc.com/culture/article/20201015-velzquezs-las-meninas-a-detail-that-decodes-a-masterpiece?ocid=ww.social.link.email.

25. Ibid.

26. Ibid.

27. Chloe Wyma, "Simone Leigh: Luhring Augustine, Chelsea," *Artforum*, November 2018, https://www.artforum.com/print/reviews/201809/simone-leigh-77366.

28. See Lisa Lowe, *The Intimacies of Four Continents* (Durham, NC: Duke University Press, 2015).

29. Deborah Gray White, *Ar'n't I a Woman? Female Slaves in the Plantation South* (New York and London: Norton, 1985), 27.

30. Ibid., 27–28.

31. Ibid., 28.

32. Ibid., 46.

33. Ibid., 49.

34. Saussure once described contemporary society's understanding of Blackness as the opposite of whiteness. Meaning that in the world in which we live, Blackness is not something organically created by a culture. Instead, it is constructed as a marker, an identity determined in opposition to an agreed upon norm or center—in this case, whiteness. In the process, constructing Blackness renders whiteness. Intended to divide, it has also become an identity to claim and willingly enter and determine by those deemed Black. By establishing differences through plantation slavery/colonial/imperial/hegemonic binaries or modernity, the significations that are generated in binary relations that interpolate gain meaning. What these meanings are is determined by those with the power to decide.

35. Sylvia Ardyn Boone, *Radiance from the Waters: Ideals of Feminine Beauty in Mende Art* (New Haven and London: Yale University Press, 1986), 15.

36. Ibid., 13.

37. Ibid., 63.

38. Ibid., 19.

39. See Louis Perrois and Charlotte Grand-Dufay, *Visions of Africa: Punu* (Milan: 5 Continents, 2008). The color white is far more nuanced in African belief systems than the manner in which it signifies race in the Americas. The Punu people of Gabon and the neighboring countries of Cameroon, Equatorial Guinea, and Congo utilize white pigments in sculpture and performance in very particular ways. In Punu, Mukudji, and Okuyi masks and reliquaries, white clay faces or skin suggest beauty. It is a type of mask once danced at all important events and can symbolize age and wisdom. These days the masks are more of a unifying symbol for the Punu people. They do not retain their full use-value. Historically, the black mask is capable of meting out justice (see page 49) and protecting the Punu from misfortune.

40. Frederick Lamp, "Art of the Baga: A Drama of Cultural Reinvention," *African Arts* 29, no. 4 (Autumn 1996): 20–33.

41. Ibid.

42. Lorraine Bangoura, "The Baga and the Inscrutable Nimba," *Negro History Bulletin* 34, no. 2 (February 1971): 32.

43. Frederick Lamp, "The Art of the Baga: A Preliminary Inquiry," *African Arts* 19, no. 2 (February 1986): 66.

44. See ibid., 66–67.

THE CLEVELAND MUSEUM OF ART BOARD OF TRUSTEES

Officers

Scott C. Mueller
Chair

Dr. William M. Griswold
Director and President, Sarah S. and Alexander M. Cutler Chair

Ellen Stirn Mavec
First Vice Chair

Virginia N. Barbato
Vice Chair

James A. Ratner
Vice Chair

Michelle Jeschelnig
Secretary

Annapurna Valluri
Treasurer and Chief Financial Officer

Russell Klimczuk
Assistant Treasurer

Stephen J. Knerly Jr.
Assistant Secretary

Standing Trustees

Stephen W. Bailey
Virginia N. Barbato
Frederick E. Bidwell
Leigh H. Carter
Reverend Dr. Jawanza K. Colvin
Sarah S. Cutler
Richard H. Fearon
Helen Forbes Fields
Lauren Rich Fine
Charlotte Fowler
Christopher Gorman
Agnes Gund
Rebecca Heller
Edward P. Hemmelgarn
Michelle Jeschelnig
Nancy F. Keithley
Douglas Kern
R. Steven Kestner
William Litzler
William P. Madar
Milton Maltz
Ellen Stirn Mavec
Scott C. Mueller
Stephen E. Myers
Katherine Templeton O'Neill
Jon H. Outcalt
Dominic L. Ozanne
Julia Pollock
Peter E. Raskind
James A. Ratner
John P. Sauerland
Manisha Sethi
Kashim Skeete
Richard P. Stovsky
Felton Thomas
Daniel P. Walsh Jr.
John Walton
Paul E. Westlake
Loyal W. Wilson

Emeritus Leadership

James T. Bartlett
Chair Emeritus

Michael J. Horvitz
Chair Emeritus

Alfred M. Rankin Jr.
Chair Emeritus

Trustees Emeriti

James T. Bartlett
James S. Berkman
Charles P. Bolton
Terrance C. Z. Egger
Robert W. Gillespie
Michael J. Horvitz
Susan Kaesgen
Robert M. Kaye
Toby Devan Lewis*
Alex Machaskee
S. Sterling McMillan III
Reverend Dr. Otis Moss Jr.
William R. Robertson
Elliott L. Schlang
David M. Schneider
Eugene Stevens

Life Trustees

Jon A. Lindseth
Mrs. Alfred M. Rankin
Donna S. Reid

Ex Officio Trustees

Susan Larson
Womens Council

Mark Deeter
Column + Stripe

Honorary Trustees

Helen Collis
Robert D. Gries
Joseph P. Keithley
Malcolm Kenney
Robert Madison
Tamar Maltz
John C. Morley
Jane Nord
Barbara S. Robinson
Iris Wolstein

as of July 2022

*Deceased

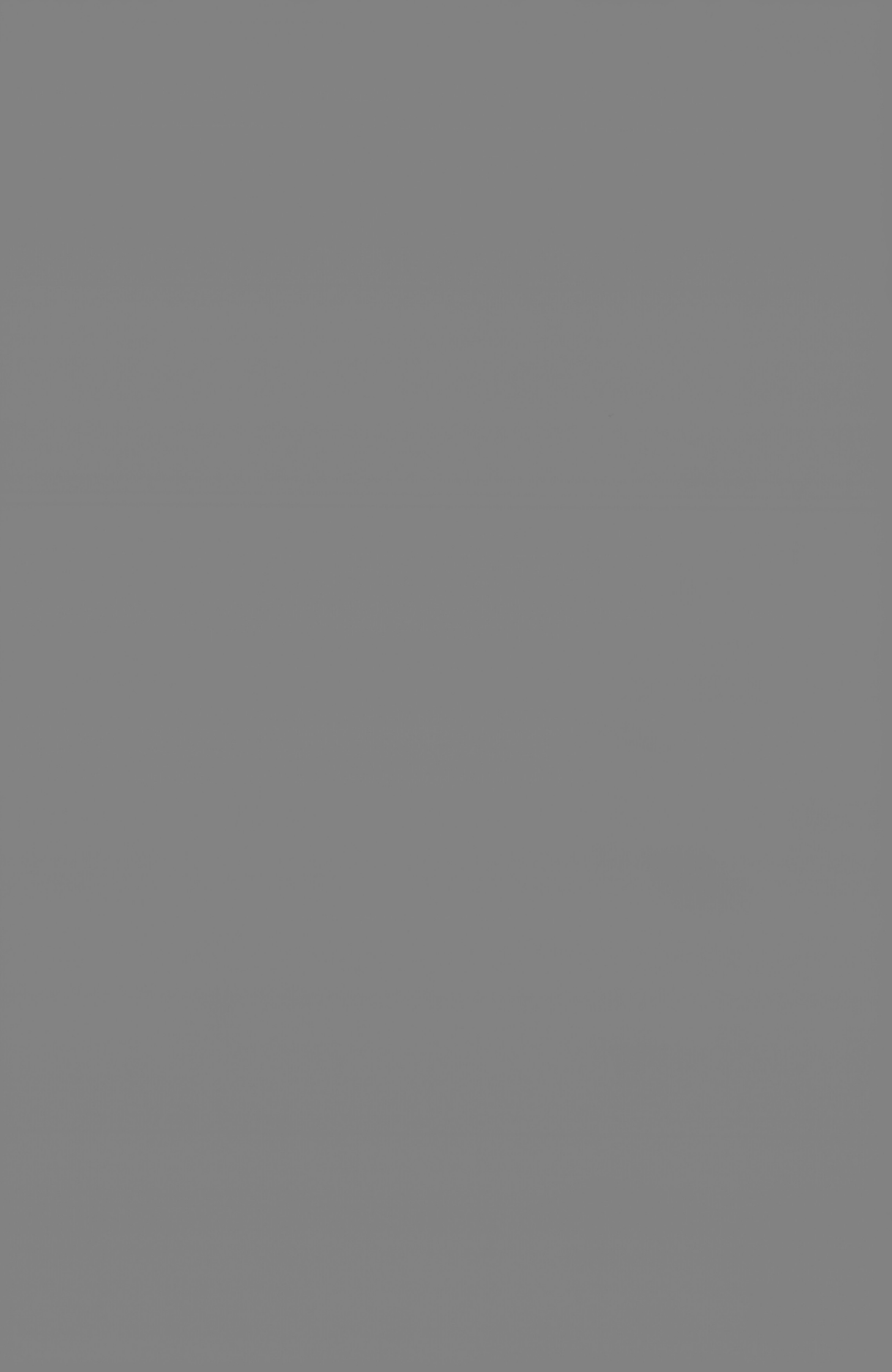